Praise for Debbie

T0032861

'Debbie is a phenomenal astrologer who has been an invaluable guide on my journey, offering unwavering support. Her insights have consistently uplifted and inspired me, making her an indispensable companion in navigating life's celestial paths.'

VEX KING, *SUNDAY TIMES* BESTSELLING AUTHOR OF *GOOD VIBES, GOOD LIFE*

'Debbie is an amazing guide and has been instrumental in helping me discover my life purpose.

ROXIE NAFOUSI, *SUNDAY TIMES* BESTSELLING AUTHOR OF *MANIFEST*

'Debbie Frank is a gifted astrologer whose experience and knowledge make her one of the best in the business. A teacher's teacher, her readings are accurate and insightful and I have no doubt that her wisdom and guidance will help readers to make smart choices about their lives.'

CHERYL RICHARDSON, *NEW YORK TIMES* BESTSELLING AUTHOR

'Debbie Frank is one of the most brilliant astrologers on the planet. She is incredibly accurate and delivers her insights in a loving yet meaningful way. Her books are wonderful and I highly recommend.'

COLETTE BARON-REID, BESTSELLING AUTHOR AND ORACLE DECK CREATOR

'Debbie is so much more than an astrologer! Her work expertly blends a wealth of astrological knowledge with deep intuitive skills. I felt amazingly seen and understood on a soul level. Pure magic.'

SOPHIE BASHFORD, AUTHOR OF *YOU ARE A GODDESS*

'At last, a new book from a master astrologer focussing on your North Node and South Node signs. This is what we've been waiting for. A true guide to your soul's astrological path from one of the world's most trusted experts.'

JESSICA ADAMS, AUTHOR AND PROFESSIONAL ASTROLOGER

'Reading Debbie Frank is like going on an archaeological dig of your soul. She helps you excavate deeper parts of yourself to access greater self-realisation. An essential tool if you have the courage to truly meet yourself.'

ANNA PASTERNAK, WRITER AND *NEW YORK TIMES* BESTSELLING AUTHOR

'This is a beautiful and easy to digest book that gives you a thorough and comprehensive understanding of how to use astrology to learn more about yourself and the blueprint of your life. A great book for beginners as well as for those with more experience in astrology to dive deeper into this ancient wisdom.'

SHEREEN ÖBERG, AUTHOR OF *THE LAW OF POSITIVISM*

'Debbie Frank's horoscopes and astrology features are always popular with *HELLO!* readers, especially her insights into the royal family's lives and relationships. Who wouldn't want to know what the stars have in store for them from Princess Diana's famed astrologer?'

HELLO! MAGAZINE

'There is no greater solace in our challenging times than to consult the Queen of the Cosmos, Debbie Frank, who seems to know where our lives are going even if we don't.'

TINA BROWN CBE, AWARD-WINNING JOURNALIST, EDITOR AND AUTHOR

'Debbie has built an amazing career reading charts for clients, helping to unlock their cosmic potential and take control of their destiny.'
TATLER MAGAZINE

'There is the sun, there is the moon, and then there is Debbie Frank. She does indeed shine bright. Full of wisdom, Debbie offers an uncanny but utterly reliable interpretation of how the cosmos is influencing your life. From love and luck to money and health, she helps you to see your path as part of a bigger journey. Her insights are incredibly helpful and positive. She's clever, warm spirited and extensively knowledgeable about astrology, an arena to which she lends credence and style. In troubled waters her words form a rock of strength and reassurance.'
DAISY FINER, FREELANCE TRAVEL JOURNALIST

'Debbie is someone who helped me get clarity and re-affirm my soul's journey. An exceptional astrologer, homeopath and energy healer. Someone who has a deep understanding of human emotions and can profoundly guide you along your emotional journey. Quite simply put, she is a beautiful soul.'
UDAY RAO, GENERAL MANAGER, FOUR SEASONS RESORTS, BALI

'My reading with Debbie was utterly transformative. Combining her true gift of intuition with accurate and insightful astrological interpretations, Debbie pinpointed and articulated many points I hadn't discussed with anyone. Where I'd previously felt unsure, I now feel empowered to move forward and choose my course of action. Debbie has made a tremendous difference in my outlook and life.'
TIFFANEY DEAGUERO, STRATEGIC GLOBAL CORPORATE EVENTS LEADER, VMWARE

Who You Came Here to Be

Who You Came Here to Be

Astrology to
Unlock Your
Cosmic Potential
and Manifest
Your Destiny

Debbie Frank

HAY HOUSE

Carlsbad, California • New York City
London • Sydney • New Delhi

Published in the United Kingdom by:
Hay House UK Ltd, The Sixth Floor, Watson House,
54 Baker Street, London W1U 7BU
Tel: +44 (0)20 3927 7290; www.hayhouse.co.uk

Published in the United States of America by:
Hay House LLC, PO Box 5100, Carlsbad, CA 92018-5100
Tel: (1) 760 431 7695 or (800) 654 5126; www.hayhouse.com

Published in Australia by:
Hay House Australia Pty Ltd, 18/36 Ralph St, Alexandria NSW 2015
Tel: (61) 2 9669 4299; www.hayhouse.com.au

Published in India by:
Hay House Publishers (India) Pvt Ltd, Muskaan Complex,
Plot No.3, B-2, Vasant Kunj, New Delhi 110 070
Tel: (91) 11 4176 1620; www.hayhouse.co.in

Text © Debbie Frank, 2021, 2024

This book was previously published as *What's Your Soul Sign?* (978-1-78817-562-3)

The moral rights of the author have been asserted.

All rights reserved. No part of this book may be reproduced by any mechanical, photographic or electronic process, or in the form of a phonographic recording; nor may it be stored in a retrieval system, transmitted or otherwise be copied for public or private use, other than for 'fair use' as brief quotations embodied in articles and reviews, without prior written permission of the publisher.

The information given in this book should not be treated as a substitute for professional medical advice; always consult a medical practitioner. Any use of information in this book is at the reader's discretion and risk. Neither the author nor the publisher can be held responsible for any loss, claim or damage arising out of the use, or misuse, of the suggestions made, the failure to take medical advice or for any material on third-party websites.

A catalogue record for this book is available from the British Library.

Tradepaper ISBN: 978-1-4019-7823-5
E-book ISBN: 978-1-83782-271-3
Audiobook ISBN: 978-1-83782-270-6

Interior illustrations: Shutterstock

This product uses responsibly sourced papers and/or recycled materials.
For more information, see www.hayhouse.co.uk.

10 9 8 7 6 5 4 3 2 1

Printed in the United States of America

This product uses responsibly sourced papers and/or recycled materials. For more information, see www.hayhouse.com.

To Lulu, my special starchild

Contents

Soul Gifts

Who am I meant to become? Why am I here? Who hasn't asked themselves those questions? They often lead to more questions, such as: Is there more to life that is beyond the physical?

I believe there is, and that if we align ourselves with the idea that we are souls, not just body parts and pieces of chemistry randomly slung together, we become aware that there is some kind of spiritual intelligence behind our existence. We can see ourselves as part of a living, intelligent cosmos, evolving in our own individual way.

A spiritually meaningful astrological perspective stems from the idea that we evolve over many lifetimes and that we come into each life with pre-agreed 'soul contracts' that are rubber-stamped with the lessons, relationships and issues that we have decided to work on. We have soul contracts with other people, with our families and co-workers. In fact, everything has meaning in terms of giving us an opportunity to learn, because we are here to grow, evolve and develop.

 We are co-creators in our lives: our souls are actively involved in the choosing of the life ingredients that will give us the lessons we agreed to learn.

It's possible our soul has chosen our celestial DNA, currently encapsulated in our genetic DNA, for our evolution. Our biology predisposes us to certain physical experiences, yet our astrology reveals our true soul intentions. If we can unlock our cosmic potential we receive higher guidance which empowers us to elevate our destiny.

Our birth chart is a detailed map of who we are and who we came here to be.

It has many layers, each one revealing more about the person we are, the person we could be and the person we're destined to be. It's all there – the things others can see about us, the things they don't know, even the things we hide from ourselves! More importantly, our birth chart reveals our true gifts, our *soul gifts*, which are just waiting to be opened...

Each planet gives us a gift, a living energy code, an intrinsic pattern that is constantly evolving as we become more aware, awake and self-empowered.

In this book, I'm offering you my own insights into how to read the celestial placements in a chart and my special secrets of how to turn these insights into incredible triggers for personal growth. I hope that as you read on, you'll see every part of your birth chart coming to life and opening up who you are in a series of exciting discoveries. These discoveries will reveal your own soul gifts and how you can use them to unlock your soul's purpose in this life-time and become who you came here to be.

Understanding the Soul Codes in Your Chart

A common misconception about astrology is that it's based on the premise that the planets make things happen. But we aren't being bombarded by malefic or benefic planets that 'do things to us'. The planets are reflecting the synchronicities of what our soul signed up for: they are the means through which we express and shape our destiny.

These signs show what we are here to experience and embody in this life. They represent the psychological and spiritual energies that we hold within us – the energies that magnetically attract the very experiences we need in order to evolve. These energies are threaded through the way we do everything, yet they also give us a vision for life in all its facets. They give us self-knowledge, yet they also take us on a journey of expansion.

In this book, we're going to explore these astrological signatures and how they appear in the birth chart – the positions of the planets and how they interact with each other to offer opportunities for personal growth and soul development.

 The placement of our planets reveals who we are on a soul level.

Most of you will be familiar with your birth sign, or Sun sign (the zodiac sign of your Sun when you are born). That piece of information alone reveals so much about you, but it's not the whole story. Here we'll start from a soul perspective, with the North and South Nodes of the Moon, which are points of karma and connection showing your soul path.

Then we'll consider the all-important access point between the cosmos and you as an individual in the form of the angles of your chart – Ascendant, Descendant, Midheaven (M/C) and Imum Coeli (I/C). These are set at the magical moment of your birth, giving you the cosmic energies that are yours to live.

Next we'll move on to discovering the secrets of all 10 planets or other celestial bodies in your chart. You'll see how these cosmic forces flow through every area of your life, from the work you do to whom you love and why, to your inner power and creative inspiration. You'll relate to how your planets are working in your life, but more importantly, you'll see how they are uniquely calibrated to magnetize the events, relationships and experiences that will help you evolve. You'll start to see the patterns and threads that weave your soul journey.

The themes of that journey are seen in the matches your personal planets – Sun, Moon, Mercury, Venus and Mars – make with the social and outer planets. These matches are known as 'aspects' and create specific themes in your life story, which are explained in more detail in Parts III and IV.

We'll look at your personal planets before moving on to the social planets, Jupiter and Saturn, which show how your destiny interacts with the wider world, then the slower-moving outer planets, Uranus, Neptune and Pluto, which describe the generational wave you are part of – your collective soul group mission. Here again, through the aspects between your inner and outer planets, you'll gain real insight into your life themes and how you can become a powerful, conscious choice-maker.

Look on the planets as a team of specialists. You wouldn't go to a brain surgeon for advice on the heart, or a barrister for guidance on your tax return. Knowing your chart's astrological codes will open your eyes to the talents, gifts and challenges in every area of your life.

***Each angle, planet or point of our chart
reveals what we have brought with us into
this lifetime and what we're here for.***

There are of course, other layers to consider in interpreting a chart – the elements (Fire, Earth, Air, Water); the houses, which are touched on here; the modalities; and more minor aspects between the celestial bodies. Astrology is a vast subject and if you wish to know more, you will find some recommendations for further reading at the back of the book.

For now, we'll focus on how to discover who you are here to become by looking at the angles, planets and points. They can take you through a portal of awareness to extraordinary personal development that could have taken decades of therapy! This book will empower you to join all the dots within yourself and to align with your innate gifts, inner guiding star and the outer cosmos to become the best *you* possible.

Is there anything more life-enhancing than knowing that you can unlock your cosmic potential and take control of your destiny?

> **Get your free birth chart at www.astro.com**

CHAPTER 1

The Magical Wisdom of Astrology

Science, sacred art, field of resonance

What can astrology teach me?
How can it help my soul development?

What does the word 'astrology' mean to you? Your 'star sign' or daily forecast? Do you know that the true magic of astrology reveals who you really are in every facet of your being? Astrology is the ultimate power tool for waking up to the world around you, transforming yourself and living at the highest vibration possible.

Are you ready to align with astrology's magical wisdom? Its signposts, messages and ongoing guidance?

 Astrology is your portal, your gateway to understanding who you really are on a soul level and who you came here to be.

Science and Sacred Art

Astrology is both a science and a sacred art. Yes, it is based on mathematically calculated alignments of the planets at a person's time, date and place of birth. Yet each chart is as individual and as full of layers as a human being. Although these days we use software to draw up a chart, the minute it's cast it constellates mystical material. So, the reading of a birth chart should be undertaken as a sacred act, never as an ego fix for knowing stuff about people. It is a way of truly understanding and appreciating the enormity and wonder of the journey of their soul.

For my own part, I have Linda Goodman to thank for sparking my passion for astrology. As a teenager reading her *Sun Signs* book, I felt that the words spoke to me, that they presented an immediately accessible insight into how people acted and felt. Now, after decades of training in all aspects of astrology, including esoteric, psychological, spiritual and medical, and decades of working as both a media and a consulting astrologer, I have built up invaluable first-hand experience of how astrology translates into life!

Knowing how a chart works has never been enough for me. Technical knowledge can't help people grow in the way that spiritual and psychological insights can. Through many years of study with extraordinary teachers and the blessing of working with thousands of clients and seeing how astrology works in practice, I have alchemized my own take on astrology as a tool for self-development and soul development.

One of the things I love most about astrology is that there's always more to learn. No matter how expert or surface your knowledge of astrology, it's a never-ending source of fascination, a labyrinth of unfolding symbolism that can be immediately understood on one level, yet yields more insights as you reflect upon it. It's so highly nuanced that one planet's core meaning can expand to resonate with literally hundreds of connections, ideas and associations.

> **Astrology itself is a field of resonance. It's both incredibly simple and incredibly complex.**

It's so much more than a few words about the day ahead. Every insight builds more layers, including the contrasts of darkness and light in a personality that paint a complete picture of that person. Except it's also an X-ray image, showing the things that *aren't* visible to the naked eye!

Since ancient times, the healing wisdom of astrology has provided guidance for the journey of the soul. Our modern-day scientific experts have largely promoted a 'rational', non-spiritual mode of existence – a world without cosmic connectedness. Yet this mode of thinking has only been prevalent for around 160 years. The wisdom of astrology far pre-dates this materialistic view of the world. Not so long ago, doctors of science were well versed in astrology as well as astronomy.

During Renaissance times, the *uomo universale* was an all-round thinker educated in all disciplines. It is only in recent times that we have been bombarded by the separated, material perspective. Yet as the planets continue to move in their courses and we continue to evolve, we are now entering a new era of consciousness where quantum science allows us to unite with a more connected universe full of frequencies, resonances and alignments. And perhaps astrology, that fascinating alchemical mixture of science and art, is finally getting its true gold moment.

How to Interpret the Birth Chart

Astrology has many layers and understanding all the ingredients in a birth chart requires a step-by-step approach. In this book, we are focusing on the meaning of the planets in the signs. However, you can start to build up a picture of how the energies of your planets blend with their setting in a particular house when you look at the wheel.

When you find your planet and houses in your own chart you will see where the energies of the planet will be active according to their house position. For example if the Moon is in your 9th house, you are very comfortable learning and travelling. If. Venus is in your 1st house, you like to create a good impression. If you would like to go further, you can look at the sections on the Social Planets (Jupiter and Saturn) and the Outer Planets (Uranus, Neptune and Pluto) and their aspects to the Personal Planets or celestial bodies (Sun, Moon, Mercury, Venus and Mars) which will give you yet another layer.

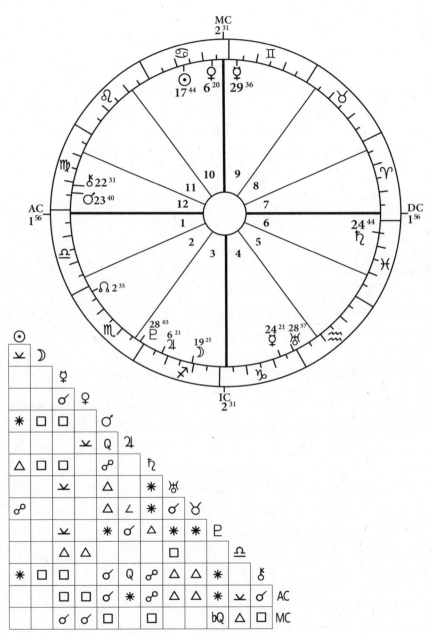

Sample birth chart for 12th July 1995, London, midday

Soul Medicine

The magical power of astrology lies in its capacity to alleviate distress through providing meaning.

If we understand that healing takes places in many areas of our life, not just our body, then astrology can be seen as giving us a toolkit to overwrite our past history with meaning, which is a miraculous way to reframe our experiences so that we get healing insights that move us beyond old issues.

This is seriously powerful. It is a way of understanding and overcoming many mental health issues. There is something about knowing that what you are going through is synchronized with the heavens that provides consolation. You aren't alone, but connected. It's such a relief to know that our experiences are not random but mirror the patterns in our birth chart. This is how my clients feel an immediate sense of connection with the cosmos. And you can too!

Our natal chart actually provides soul medicine by revealing why we go through significant emotional challenges, events, problems and issues that may be very different from other people's life experiences. What is it about us that draws these in? Why do we attract them? The Law of Attraction may be one form of explanation, but it doesn't get to the underlying reason why we may struggle to have the life we desire. This is because our ego is in competition with our soul to control the direction of our life. We have a karmic purpose that may be very different from how our ego would like to live.

Our Ascendant and planetary signs may serve up immediately recognizable experiences. It can be as simple as Venus in Libra loving beauty, or Mars in Aries being highly competitive, yet if we delve deeper, we reach a vast reservoir of nuance that tells us the soul intention of Venus in Libra is to consciously connect with others in a graceful way, whilst the soul purpose of Mars in Aries might be to courageously take on a huge challenge. One person might have both these factors in their chart, creating one of those contradictions that are the stuff of human nature and the soul's multifaceted purpose.

Then there is the dynamic between the ego and the soul, which operate on different levels and with entirely different understandings of what's important in life. Yet once we get hold of the idea that we are a soul encountering experiences for a meaningful purpose, we begin to see how one-dimensional the ego is. It can't grasp the majesty of a period of initiation, for example, because it's so busy seeking to satisfy its desires.

There are so many healing insights to be found in astrology and my hope is that you will gain numerous insights into your own soul journey and how the magic of astrology can enable you to transform your hot-spots, understand what makes you and others tick and live at the highest possible frequency!

> *Everyone has a celestial blueprint, a divine design, a perfectly put-together plan that is calibrated with the planets to deliver the most incredible synchronicity.*

So, let's discover yours...

If you haven't already got your free birth chart, please go to www.astro.com

Now let's dive in and see how every part of your birth chart comes to life and reveals who you came here to be.

CHAPTER 2

Nodes

Spiritual databank and way forward

What is my soul path?
What am I here to give and what am I here to learn?

The North Node (♌ in your chart) and the South Node (☋ in your chart) of the Moon aren't physical bodies, but two points that mark the crossings of the Moon in its orbital path. They hold a special vibrational frequency and give us clues to what we've encountered in other lifetimes and are here to learn in this one.

The two points are always in opposite signs, creating a polarity, a stretch between our comfort zone and our need to develop more. These pulse points hold the memories of past lives and the soul contract for this life.

The sign of the South Node shows what we've already stored in our spiritual databank, what we have come in with and have available to us as an inbuilt resource.

*__The sign of the North Node describes what
we are aiming towards in this lifetime.__*

South Node energies are familiar to us and we sink back into them and can access them with ease. But if we continue with this way of behaving, we get stuck in repeating the South Node pattern, which limits our growth. When we step into the North Node way of behaving, on the other hand, we feel released from our past and start our personal and soul development. What we really need to do is create a sense of balance between the Node energies, so that we integrate the past with the future.

Soul Connections

When our South Node conjuncts another person's planets or points, there will be an immediate sense of connection. This could be a past-life connection, a sense of something familiar and shared, and a glimpse of being brought together as part of a soul family. When it is our North Node that is activated by another person's planets or points, then that person will show us how to take the next steps towards fulfilling our soul purpose. They may play a pivotal role in our life that takes us beyond our comfort zone. This connection also has a fated quality.

Getting to Know Your Nodes

Find your North Node (☊) and its opposite point, the South Node (☋), in your birth chart. They will fall in opposite signs, creating a special affinity with these opposite energies in your life. Bringing them into balance is a beautiful thing for your soul growth and personal evolution.

North Node in Aries–South Node in Libra
You enjoy harmony, peace and cooperation, but need to learn how to act independently and do your own thing. You aspire to be assertive and go-getting rather than accommodating other people's needs and wishes.

North Node in Libra–South Node in Aries
You're not short of fiery spark and can get things off the ground by yourself, yet your soul lesson is to collaborate with others in a harmonious way. It's important to look for peace and harmony in relationships rather than assert yourself.

North Node in Taurus–South Node in Scorpio
Your penetrating insight and capacity to rise like a phoenix from the ashes when crisis hits is to be offset by keeping things simple and secure. You need to build things up for the long term and focus on sustainability.

North Node in Scorpio–South Node in Taurus
You're attached to keeping things the way they are. Good at hanging in there, you have inbuilt endurance. Yet your soul message is to take on things that will change your life and enable you to develop greater awareness.

North Node in Gemini–South Node in Sagittarius
Your innately philosophical nature and capacity to see the bigger picture now need to be honed into communication and people skills. You're at home in the world, enjoying a broad spectrum of

cultures and ideologies, yet this time around it's all about sending the message out.

North Node in Sagittarius–South Node in Gemini

Your natural curiosity about people and ideas means you easily assimilate knowledge and information. Now it's time to turn that into something meaningful. Travel, education and adventure will lead to greater understanding.

North Node in Cancer–South Node in Capricorn

You're naturally attuned to taking on responsibilities and being self-disciplined. Self-reliant and capable of sustained effort and hard work, you could benefit from turning your attention towards emotions and emotional attachments. Being practical must be balanced with coming from the heart.

North Node in Capricorn–South Node in Cancer

Your emotional issues and attachments can be brought into balance by developing greater self-reliance. Looking after others or being looked after is a dependency net that prevents you from feeling successful in your own right. Learning detachment and resilience brings personal growth.

North Node in Leo–South Node in Aquarius

You have a humanitarian bent, a capacity to think beyond yourself and align yourself with groups who collaborate for the greater good. Yet you need to develop your own personal flair and confidence and present your unique qualities with style and radiance.

North Node in Aquarius–South Node in Leo

It's easy for you to tune in to your own vision of how things should be. You have a certain style and dramatic flair. Yet it's important to develop the capacity to become part of something bigger than you, to collaborate with others or to envisage projects that will help others.

North Node in Pisces–South Node in Virgo

Your attention to detail and powers of observation keep your personal standards very high. Well-organized and efficient, you know how to create order. Allowing yourself to go with the flow, follow your intuition and dip into your imagination will enable you to create something even better.

North Node in Virgo–South Node in Pisces

Nothing fazes you, as your wide-angle lens on life refuses to get caught up in the noise. You have a spiritual and creative well of intuition to guide you. Yet you will benefit from a more targeted approach. Hard work is the antidote to purposeless dreaming.

CHAPTER 3

Angles

*The meet-and-greet intersection
between the soul and the cosmos*

How do I interact with the world?
What is my window on the world?

The reason why our time of birth is so important in astrology is because it's a huge metaphysical moment – the moment when we, as a spiritual soul, enter our earthly body and the cosmos breathes life into our journey here on Earth.

Our birth chart is calculated according to the time, date and place of birth. Remember to download yours at **www.astro.com** The time of birth is what sets the angles, creating four important life points, the Ascendant, Descendant, Midheaven and Imum Coeli, which are formed from two pairs of opposite signs. Opposite signs always contain the exact opposite qualities and ingredients. The tension between them forms the stretched canvas on which the colour of our planets can be seen.

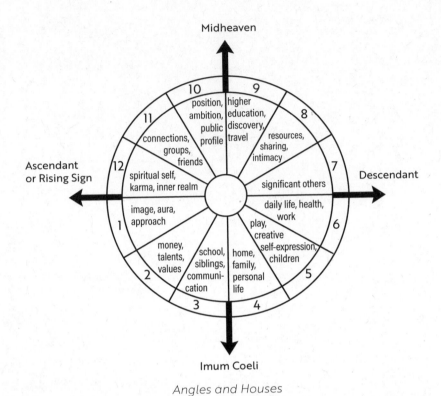

Angles and Houses

Your planets will be positioned in one of the 12 houses.

Your birth time creates your map. Your angles set the structure for the 12 houses. Your Ascendant or Rising Sign begins the 1st house, which follows through to the 4th House that starts with your Imum Coeli. Then your Descendant fixes the point of your 7th house, following on to the 10th house, which marks the start of your Midheaven.

Take a look at your own birth chart (you can obtain yours for free at ***www.astro.com***). Your planets will be positioned in one of the 12 houses – the segments within the wheel of the chart.

The illustration on the previous page shows the houses of our birth chart and their related meanings. It is within these specific areas of life that our planets play out. We can imagine the wheel of our birth chart to be like the London Eye, with our vantage point being set by our birth time.

Our birth time creates our window on the world. The angles shape our reality and provide our ongoing interface with the world.

It's as if our birth moment sets off a ripple effect that runs through the rest of our life. It sets the angles, and these describe how our soul intersects with our ego life and all we meet within it.

Let's look at your angles now and how they frame your life:

- What do you give out? (Ascendant/Rising Sign – ASC)
- Whom do you draw in? (Descendant – DESC)
- Where are you going? (Midheaven – M/C)
- Where are you coming from? (Imum Coeli – I/C)

Ascendant/Rising Sign

What Do You Give Out?

***Birth, the entry point to anything in
life, persona, navigator, appearance,
how your soul expresses you.***

Sometimes known as your rising sign, this point is the sign that is rising in the east at the moment of your first breath. Your astral body enters first, carrying the soul codes of this life with this first breath, so it marks the beginning of your incarnation. With this breath, the stage is set via the chart wheel, placing the planets in position for the unfolding of your destiny.

Great currents of spiritual energy are thought to flow along the horizon, and the all-important moment of your birth provides your personal horizon. Your rising sign describes how you look, present yourself and appear to the world – you are likely to have a body type similar to your Ascendant. However your Ascendant not only describes how you look, but how the world looks to your eyes.

***You view the world through the lens
of your Ascendant sign.***

So, your Ascendant shows how you meet and greet the world on an ongoing basis, how you move into something new and how you interpret reality.

Descendant

Whom Do You Draw In?

> *Significant others, relationships, business and personal partnerships, your interface with the public, what your soul draws to you.*

This point lies opposite to your rising sign and there is a real sense that whatever you're putting out on the Ascendant, you're receiving counter-balancing energy through the significant others on your life path, as shown by the Descendant. The Descendant crosses the chart at the cusp of the seventh house, which is your partnership point, where you draw in significant others, be they business or personal.

> *You give out at the Ascendant and pull in at the Descendant.*

This is where the persona that expresses your individual self in the first house has to negotiate with other people's needs and wishes. It can also describe your relationship with the public.

Of course, the actual angle is in *your* chart – you are attracting these qualities into your life. Your relationships can be seen as a projection of what's in your chart. Sometimes the people you magnetize into your life through the frequency of your Descendant very clearly have planets in the sign that is found here. We attract those who resonate with our Descendant in order to transform, grow and reach our soul potential.

Ascendant–Descendant Dynamics

So, what kind of self–other pattern and magnetic pull do you have going on in your chart? Your Ascendant–Descendant axis is super-important in terms of representing your personal Law of Attraction. The signs here are always opposite to each other, but with conscious awareness, we see that they are linked. They balance each other perfectly and each represents the hidden qualities of the other.

Aries–Libra Dynamic ♈ ♎

Is it me-me-me or we-we-we? This polarity on the axis of self-versus-relationship intensifies the balancing act between independence and co-operation. Between self and partnership. With Aries and Libra here, there is often a big life lesson in the art of relationship versus the needs of the self. Relationships can be your biggest catalysts for change.

Aries on the Ascendant–Libra on the Descendant

Aries is a warrior, so your take on the world is that it's a competitive arena where you have to move fast and conquer. You love to be first in or to do a start-up, and your pushiness gets you through most doors whilst others have to wait. You adore challenges that are full of fire and colour, and you'll never take 'no' for an answer. Your mission is to initiate. You possess great personal energy and courage and work best independently.

With Libra on the Descendant, your feisty nature tends to attract those who need you to lead. Your partner is likely to be cooperative, diplomatic and interested in maintaining peace in the relationship, whilst you are the driving force.

Libra on the Ascendant–Aries on the Descendant
Libra is a charmer, a neutralizer, a negotiator, so your approach to the world is to manage everything with grace, courtesy and finesse. You dislike confrontation and can find a million ways to appease others and avoid burning bridges or stirring up a storm. Aesthetics and social skills are your stock in trade. Your mission is to create harmony. You possess style, diplomacy and an innate desire for fairness.

You are attracted to more dominant partners and enjoy the spark they bring in terms of lighting up your life. That is, unless the connection turns into fireworks at every opportunity, which you find destabilizes your delicate balance. Whatever the situation, you spend a lot of time working out the give-and-take of a relationship.

Taurus–Scorpio Dynamic ♉ ♏

Both Taurus and Scorpio are signs that explore the realm of attachment, Taurus at the more material end and Scorpio the deeply personal. Life themes for both revolve around permanence and transformation. Therefore, with this Ascendant–Descendant axis, issues of holding on and letting go come up in your approach to life and partnership.

Taurus on the Ascendant–Scorpio on the Descendant
Slow and steady does it with Taurus rising. You possess patience and practicality and a reassuring touch that enables others to place their trust in you. You like to build things slowly, to invest your energy in long-term results. Your mission is to hold things together. To be a rock for others.

With Scorpio on the relationship angle of your chart, you magnetize intense experiences through partnerships. Through them, you enter the realm of passion and complexity, and you may even have a liking for those who live by different values or teeter on the dark side. You are likely to draw people with complex soul issues and emotional histories in order to balance your inherent attachment to simplicity.

Scorpio on the Ascendant–Taurus on the Descendant
You're 007, giving little away! Yet your aura exudes knowingness. You may have been born into complex emotional dynamics or an atmosphere of trauma. Possibly a death or significant ending accompanied your birth. You tend to stay private or under the radar, sensing that full self-expression might give too much away. Your soul sign message is to transform yourself and others through understanding the deeper nuances of life. Passion and intensity are your soul gifts, but you are capable of holding them within.

Stability in relationships provides the perfect balance for your deeply emotional nature and you call in partners who are the rock to your bombshell! You value long-lasting attachments and dependability that earth and ground you. Your soul work is to learn to hold on to inner security whilst at the same time going through your birth-death-rebirth cycles!

Gemini–Sagittarius Dynamic ♊ ♐

This axis is all about communication, education, movement and travel. You are constantly being pulled to know more, see more, connect more. Lively and on the go, you dislike anything static or limiting, so relationships have to offer growth and learning, otherwise you will move on.

Gemini on the Ascendant–Sagittarius on the Descendant
Inquisitive and restless, you are a great communicator and people person, constantly multitasking and flitting between subjects and activities. A strong interest in life creates a youthful energy at any age and an ability to connect across any divide. On a soul level, you need to get your message across, to broadcast information and create points of interest.

With Sagittarius on the Descendant, you are drawn to the meaning of life, rather than pure information. You may attract someone who broadens your knowledge or understanding of life through another culture. The partnership itself needs to keep evolving to maintain your interest.

Sagittarius on the Ascendant–Gemini on the Descendant
With Sagittarius rising, you greet the world with a great deal of enthusiasm and warmth. There is an openness and good humour about this Jupiter-ruled sign and often a larger-than-life quality. Travel often features highly, as you like to connect globally and explore what the world has to offer. On a soul level, you can uplift others with your positive energy and help them see beyond limitations.

Gemini on the Descendant can give multiple choice in partnerships! There may be a need for constant stimulation that one person alone might find hard to provide. Communication and a meeting of minds are key to the success of your relationships.

Cancer–Capricorn Dynamic ♋ ♑

This pair of signs across the Ascendant–Descendant suggests that taking care of people and establishing security in personal relationships and in life are paramount. It is a heart–head dynamic where feelings and practicality have to be balanced. Often parenting themes come up strongly in relationships, with one person providing guidance and nurturing to the other. There can also be a conflict between controlling your feelings and expressing them.

Cancer on the Ascendant–Capricorn on the Descendant

You meet the world with emotional sensitivity and empathy and find ways to look after other people on an emotional, caring level. You have a soul connection to the Great Mother – you intuitively know what is needed and what to give in any situation. Yet your affinity with the Moon means your own fluctuating feelings pull you in and out of your shell.

With Capricorn on the Descendant, you have a need to balance your emotional responses with practicality and groundedness imported from others. You are likely to attract those who pull you down to earth. Karmic lessons can be a strong part of the relationship picture, too, as Capricorn is ruled by Saturn, planet of soul karma.

Capricorn on the Ascendant–Cancer on the Descendant

You are primarily responsible and mature from your early years. You take life seriously and work hard at establishing your place in the world. You take note of hierarchies and levels, in keeping with the climb of the mountain goat, and tend to pick your way slowly and cautiously towards your goal. On a soul level, you are here to learn self-sufficiency.

With Cancer on the partnership angle of your chart, you tend to draw people who are in touch with their feelings in order to balance your own practical outlook. The home, family life and building a permanent union are important to you, and the ties that bind are very binding indeed.

Leo–Aquarius Dynamic ♌ ♒

When Leo and Aquarius run across the Ascendant–Descendant axis, there is a need to integrate the ego self with greater objectivity. Leo has a creative showiness, whereas Aquarius stands back to observe the whole. Leo places heartfelt love above all; Aquarius is concerned with ideas, friendly interaction and humanity. The nature and expression of love is a theme here, with a clash between the personal and impersonal, attached and detached.

Aquarius on the Ascendant–Leo on the Descendant
With lofty Aquarius on the Ascendant, you have an air of detached friendliness and a concern for humanity that defaults to a cool position rather than a special need. Your ideals about human behaviour can be hard to integrate into the realm of intimacy. Your soul growth requires you to balance heart and head.

With Leo on the Descendant, the attraction is to those who rise and shine. You are magnetically drawn towards heart-centred types and your soul lesson is how to give attention to a partnership whilst satisfying your need for other interactions in the world.

Leo on the Ascendant–Aquarius on the Descendant
You are a natural-born star. You light up a room, exude charisma, draw attention and give your heart and soul. You have a highly developed sense of self, which can be perceived as selfish until the

focus comes from the heart. Your soul lesson is to move from self-centred to giver from the heart.

With cool Aquarius on the Descendant, you attract partners who are unwilling to play the rapturous audience and who challenge you to think differently. Your partnership frequency is quirky, unusual and not given to great shows of emotion, so balancing heart and head, love and logic, is the soul lesson of this axis.

Virgo–Pisces Dynamic ♍ ♓

When Virgo and Pisces flank the Ascendant–Descendant axis, the chief issue is control versus chaos! This is often an important theme in relationships, with one person having a marked effect on the other's *modus operandi*. Intuition and creativity are the domain of Pisces, whilst order and management are that of Virgo. Polar opposites – but when balanced, they can manifest amazing dreams.

Virgo on the Ascendant–Pisces on the Descendant

You are a neat-nick with a critical and discerning eye that differentiates, curates, organizes and solves problems. You're a planner who needs to maintain control and sort things out, right down to the smallest details. At a soul level, you meet the world with a humble, service-oriented approach.

With Pisces on the Descendant, you magnetize a 'floatier' partner – a dreamer, an idealist, a romantic. Then you get easily caught up in trying to 'fix' or clear up after them or keep the wheels of the relationship turning. This frequency can draw a variety of partners and experiences, including a true soul-mate, a creative, an addict and unrequited love.

Pisces on the Ascendant–Virgo on the Descendant

You see the world through an ethereal, magical lens. Often creative, dreamy, sensitive and otherworldly, you are in tune with the subtle levels of life and can be overly open to currents in the atmosphere and easily hurt. Your soul lesson is to avoid using your chameleon-like energy to turn yourself into what others want you to be.

With Virgo on the Descendant, you attract a partner who brings a level of earthiness to the relationship. This organized partnership frequency offsets your passivity, your desire to live a rarified life rather than get your hands dirty with the daily grind. It can be a magical combination or a constant adjustment.

Midheaven (M/C)

Where Are You Going?

 Your prime time, profile, role in the world, public face, persona and identity; how you set your destiny.

The Midheaven or M/C is the highest point (midday point) in the chart. It shows what your soul is reaching for. What you are known for. The qualities of the sign here are immediately visible to others, as you put them out there in the world. You want to be seen and to achieve in this particular way. So, the Midheaven can be both your career path and any other external status (including marital), your position in life or a label you have. It correlates to where you wish to go in life, what you want to achieve.

The Imum Coeli (I/C)
Where Are You Coming From?

*The inner you, the internal world, home,
family, ancestry, personal realm.*

The Imum Coeli or I/C is the midnight point – it is your deep ancestral past, life heritage, background and what you came in with, not only your family of origin but even what you have learned in a past life. The sign on the I/C relates to who you are on the inside. Also, your home and roots. This part of the chart is connected to your personal development, spiritual work and who you are at home or in private. So the sign on this angle of the chart isn't visible to all and sundry, only to those who live with you or know the private you.

M/C–I/C Dynamics

Again, as with the opposing signs on our Ascendant–Descendant axis, we have a pair of opposite signs on the vertical axis of our birth chart. What we put out at the top of our chart, the peak, is inextricably linked to who we are at the base camp of the I/C. This axis reveals so much about our soul's intention (M/C) and our personal heritage and karma (I/C). When we balance the expression of these signs, we feel our energies are fully turned on. We can see where we've been and what we could be, and we can live from the highest vibration of our soul.

Aries–Libra ♈ ♎

Aries on the M/C–Libra on the I/C

The sign of the warrior on the Midheaven engages the spirit of enterprise. You do best when you act independently, go it alone and do your own thing. Aries is an initiator and highly competitive, yet spiritually you are engaging with the art of war, strategizing how to get ahead and win. You want to push forward, but need to engage your higher will and learn when to act and when to stand back.

Libra on the I/C suggests a past life where aesthetics and socializing played an important role. They may continue to do so. Your home is likely to be a place of beauty and peace. Harmony is your inner compass point.

Libra on the M/C–Aries on the I/C

With Libra on the Midheaven, you are a strategist and negotiator in all you do. Art, beauty and aesthetics are points of interest and you have a strong need to partner or collaborate with others. You dislike conflict and avoid 'uncivilized' behaviour, preferring to keep your world as graceful and elegant as possible.

With Aries on the I/C, there could be fireworks on the home front or within your family of origin. You come from a past life or ancestry of activity, possibly involving fighting or defending home territory. Highly active in your personal, home and family life, you are the person who makes things happen.

Taurus–Scorpio ♉ ♏

Taurus on the M/C–Scorpio on the I/C

With Taurus on the Midheaven, you are a steady builder, achieving your goals slowly but surely. Your relationship to the earthly realm, including nature and the body, is very important to you. Taurus also has a grip on resources and money, so you have a good business head, but tend to get distracted by life's pleasures. The arts and beauty are your pathways to success.

Scorpio on the I/C suggests a complex ancestral or family history. It can be hard for you to let go, as you may have an intense attachment to the story, but your soul path is to transform like the mythical phoenix rising from the ashes.

Scorpio on the M/C–Taurus on the I/C

When the intense sign of Scorpio is on the Midheaven, the drive to achieve can be all-consuming, or the path to success can require you to transform yourself or to engage with a soul mission of transforming the world. Scorpio's depth aligns with exposing or working with the more shadowy aspects of life, too. Basically, you can't just have a 'day job' – it has to be deep and meaningful.

Taurus on the I/C is the 'home comforts' signature. You value security and stability and have a long-lasting attachment to home, family and nature. This is the firmly rooted family tree.

Gemini–Sagittarius ♊ ♐

Gemini on the M/C–Sagittarius on the I/C

Up on the Midheaven, the multiplicity of Gemini lends itself to lots of talents, aims and ambitions. You could have several businesses or plans going on at once. You have versatility and adaptability, but essentially you are all about communication and connection. You are great at selling ideas, news and information, and at negotiation and trading. Your need for stimulation keeps you on the move.

With Sagittarius on the I/C, you have an adventurous spirit, a sense of wanting to live life on a broad canvas. You might come from a family where education, religion, spirituality or travel were important. Personal growth and an optimistic attitude are your soul codes.

Sagittarius on the M/C–Gemini on the I/C

With Sagittarius on the Midheaven, you have big ambitions and a global vision – a desire to push forward and reach far and wide. You spread your message across all available channels and infuse others with your enthusiasm. Whatever your line of business, there is a teacher within you and it's easy for you to make global connections.

Gemini on the I/C suggests a home life that buzzes with the desire to communicate, learn, exchange and interact with others. For this reason, you like to keep on the move, or at least very busy. Education is often a big family value and there's the possibility of more than one home or a blended family.

Cancer–Capricorn ♋ ♑

Cancer on the M/C–Capricorn on the I/C

With Cancer on the Midheaven, your approach to what you want to achieve in life is based on feelings and intuition rather than logic. You have an innate instinct for looking after others, which may be your career or just the way you engage with the world. Either way, Cancerian emotional intelligence and sensitivity to others are channelled into how you move towards your goals.

Capricorn on the I/C suggests a huge drive for security, both material and emotional. However, your early years or the family legacy may be of the 'tough love' variety. It may also be that circumstances require you to stand on your own two feet. You take responsibility for others and can carry a lot on your shoulders, but you learn to relax in your later years.

Capricorn on the M/C–Cancer on the I/C

With the most professional of signs on the Midheaven, you yearn for professional respect. You are someone who adheres to the rules of conduct and can be a high-achiever with a 'top job' managing others or heading up a business. You're prepared to put in the hours and pride yourself on working hard, no matter what. Others acknowledge this and rely on you to hold things together.

Cancer on the I/C shows a real nesting instinct. Your home life underpins your world. You like to nurture others and know how to channel divine mother energy. Family-minded, you wish to create a sense of belonging and security, and your home provides a safe space away from the outside world.

Leo–Aquarius ♌ ♒

Leo on the M/C–Aquarius on the I/C

Leo is the sign that likes to shine, so whatever you do in the outside world, you tend to engage with it creatively and charismatically, drawing a lot of attention. You have your own personal sense of quality and style. This is your trademark. It can be part of your personal brand. Your superstar ambitions need an outlet!

With Aquarius on the I/C, you are quite capable of stepping outside traditional family life. You may create an unusual home, and certainly personal freedom and independence are important to you. You are a maverick who doesn't see the need to conform to what others view as 'security'.

Aquarius on the M/C–Leo on the I/C

The sign of Aquarius on the M/C suggests you enjoy work that connects you to causes or technologies that can make the world a better place. You have a humanitarian vision that enables you to stand out from the old world order and ways. You may be an outlier or an activist or simply enjoy pursuing the new.

With Leo on the I/C, you like to create an air of specialness in your home life. A marked sense of style underpins the way you live and you exude warmth and generosity towards those who are close to you or under your wing.

Virgo–Pisces ♍ ♓

Virgo on the M/C–Pisces on the I/C

You go about things with precision and possess a high degree of perfectionism. Communication and organization engage you – you do like to keep the information flowing and the administration working perfectly. Your critical eye can also make you feel as if you could do better. Virgo is modest and service-oriented.

Pisces on the I/C suggests that your early years may involve you having to adapt and adjust. Creativity, sacrifice and a loose structure can all be themes. Your soul is searching for inner peace and enlightenment; you have a desire to be on the spiritual path. Finding the ideal home or spiritual home is another longing.

Pisces on the M/C–Virgo on the I/C

You're looking for a role that transcends the mundane. This might lead to creative or artistic endeavours, helping others or entering the music business. Anything that is involved with images, be it fashion, film or photography, can bring out your Piscean capacity to create something special. However, your work might lead you to give a lot of yourself, perhaps more than you anticipated.

With Virgo on the I/C, you like to have a solid base that runs like clockwork. Again, you might expect a lot of yourself here and be running around after others. Your early life may have emphasized academic achievement and fostered a perfectionist streak that is hard to drop. On a soul level, you are being encouraged to serve others, which is a higher vibration than enslaving yourself!

Part II

The Personal Planets

The Sun, Moon, Mercury, Venus and Mars activate our primary personal energies. The Sun and Moon are luminaries rather than planets but, due to their personal nature in astrology, are grouped with the personal planets. The signs they are in create our individual signature. We might have our Sun in steady Taurus, for example, our Moon in impulsive Aries, our Venus in social butterfly Gemini and our Mars in intensely focused Scorpio.

The placements of these personal planets are the ingredients of the fascinating individual recipe we have chosen to make in our life.

Finding Your Personal Planets

Take a look at the personal planets in your own chart (you can obtain yours from **www.astro.com** for free). Your personal planets will be positioned in one of the 12 houses according to your time of birth which determines the positions of all the angles, planets and houses.

The personal planets hold the essential blueprint of who you came here to be.

CHAPTER 4

Sun

*Core self, king, yang, masculine
energy, ego, higher self*

Who am I?
What is my special power?

Think for a second about the sheer life-giving properties of the Sun. Without the Sun, we wouldn't exist. It sustains us with light and warmth, radiating its life-force and offering us a new dawn every day, as well as precious vitamin D3. Individually, our solar spark is our *chi*, our life-force, a micro-bite taken from the Sun's glow that revitalizes and energizes us.

 **If you want to find the essence of who you came
here to be, look at the position of the Sun which
is the flag-bearer for your primary frequency.**

In our chart, the Sun (☉) is absolutely *numero uno*. In the same way as the Sun's rays physically shine across the world, reaching everybody, its natural forces symbolize how we individually shine our light by radiating warmth and self-expression. The Sun shows us our special power, life path and soul development in the form of the hero archetype. We are on a hero's journey - a great adventure.

Who Could We Be?

The Sun is essentially the unifying force that holds all the keys to our soul's development through our life journey.

The Sun's sign points us towards our personal quest or challenge, but we don't get there all in one go, and we are not born fully downloaded, fully fledged into our Sun sign. We get shy Leos and out-of-balance Librans because the Sun is what we need to develop in this lifetime. It holds the main plotline of our story.

The Sun holds the potential for our 'best bits'. It is who we could be!

This can take a lifetime as self-awareness downloads incrementally or we can receive an early wake-up call.

However it happens, when we live our full potential at its highest frequency, we are literally lit up by the light that pulses through our Sun sign, giving us a great infusion of inner life-force. We're able to meet a challenge, overcome an obstacle or change an old pattern. At a high frequency, the Sun is a constant stream of inner light.

If we remain unconscious or undeveloped, then our true self, symbolized by our Sun, lies dormant and we don't get to know who we really are. We repeatedly go back to sleep, even though the Sun is asking us to express the power of the self. But being an empty shell is far from an ideal state.

> ***We need to find out who we are, not who others***
> ***think we are, or what we were born into.***

In this life, we are a spirit in a material world. We are also a soul with an ego; we have a higher and a lower nature. On top of differentiating ourselves from others, our Sun sign shows us both our personality in the form of the small ego and the eternal soul self or Higher Self.

The way the mainstream is constructed means we are asked to align with tick-box labels such as our marital status, job, educational credentials, and so on. It's easy to define ourselves like this. But if we experience any kind of change in our external set-up, the small ego is sent into a spin. The ego constantly tries to defend against any kind of humiliation or loss. The big cosmic joke is that the ego is bound to lose the power battle at some point, so it's good to have ourselves sorted out on the inside, which is where our special power lies.

The Sun is yang, masculine energy, and no matter which sex or orientation we are, we need to find this vital strength in ourselves and discover who we really are.

Who Is Living This Life?

In this life, our emotional body and small ego can feel injured and insulted by other people's actions. The ego in particular suffers from indignation in its desire to have full power and control over life, because inevitably we don't get what we want all the time.

The ego makes a big fuss, but if we come from the light force of our Sun, we eventually realize we've had enough of the small ego's demands. We realize that we do have the power to make choices. We cultivate our Higher Self or soul presence, which possesses grace, detachment and peace, rather than our ego, which throws its toys out of the pram when life is unfair.

It is duality that gives us pain and a sense of separation. The concept of light and dark, Sun and Shadow, revolves around duality. The big reveal is when we know what's true for us and we know who we are on the inside, not the outside. Any darkness experienced is then accepted as merely part of the journey. Less-than-perfect situations are embraced, even though they seem contrary to our wellbeing, and the contradiction itself is accepted.

Getting to this point is what makes us a powerful soul. We learn to shift our perception to overcome the duality. We learn to shadow-dance and accept the darkness. We stop struggling. We stop creating personal stories that feed us with lack of power, or responsibility, or feed us pain. The ego likes to generate these stories to maintain the psychic virus that tells us we are a victim and we need x, y or z.

 In fact, we have a beautiful destiny that is totally independent of anything the ego wants.

Going a bit deeper, we can ask, 'Who is it that's living this life? Who's running the show? Is it our soul or our ego?'

How Can We Heal and Light Up?

Can we be happy regardless of what is happening? Can we be still in the midst of turmoil? The Sun holds the healing power of inner light, no matter what's going on.

 We can make the choice to be a light warrior.

Dropping the expectations and conditions of the lower self (the survival instincts of the lower-frequency ego) immediately sets us free. We have the power to stop making everything about us, to stop taking everything personally and to reduce the level of 'personality clutter' that stems from the little ego. If we can find a way to stop creating drama and just slow our breathing, we have space. And freedom. We can begin to witness what's going on instead of reacting to it, being triggered and involved, thinking that it's such a big deal. We can remove ourselves from the stress response.

This in itself is healing, but the biggest healing in life is finding what lights us up. Our Sun sign is the biggest clue. It shows what kind of medicine we need to heal and repair ourselves. How we can develop a meaningful sense of self. How we can experience more love, more creativity and optimism.

If our life-force is weakened because our ego is not fully incarnated in our body, then we tend to get trampled on both by life's events and other people. The healthy ego forms an inner sense of self that doesn't look for external things to either define or fulfil it, because there's a true sense of self that connects to the core being.

If we never find the light inside ourselves then we are living with a weak Sun (or ego) that is struggling both emotionally and physically. Being *selfish* gets a bad rap, but our health, happiness and wellbeing depend on having a strong sense of self. This includes having boundaries that protect the self, yet being able to self-express, rather than self-repress.

Connecting to our Higher Self is also central to our development, particularly the high-vibration kind. Our Sun holds the intentions of our soul or Higher Self, acting like a personal GPS system or guiding light that directs us to where we need to go. This might not tally with where our lesser ego wants to take us!

Our childhood development unfolds in seven-year stages and we pass through phases of emotional, mental and psycho-spiritual development that should result in maturity at 28/29. We may need to retrospectively heal some of these developmental stages if we didn't receive early nurturing from our parents or weren't guided and protected in childhood. Some of us remain frozen in various stages, but the good news is that we can still grow into our true identity later in life.

A healthy Sun and strong self mean we are less prone to being invaded, manipulated or led off-track. We all live in the quantum field and therefore our energies and frequencies mingle and we are constantly picking up signals, emotions and unconscious energies from other people that have positive or negative effects. If we merge too much, or have a compulsive desire to be liked, then our core sense of self begins to blend into the selves of others. Then we literally don't know who we are and become imprinted with other people's needs, wishes and desires. So, staying clear in our Sun energy is vital.

Physically, a weakened ego means we are less robust. For a start, we find it harder to warm our blood. Without strong energy in our ego and heart, we are more susceptible to poor circulation, weakened heart vitality, depression or autoimmune diseases. It is also the ego that connects to the life of our individual cells, with powers to strengthen our immunity by recognizing the invasion of foreign bodies or when our own cells must be naturally replaced.

The Sun is the channel that moves the vitality from the spiritual world into our body. It rules the physical heart and we can invite powerful, warm healing ego forces into our heart at any time. We can salute the Sun in yoga pose, or connect to the Sun force by bowing to the Sun at sunrise. The heart is a central force for transformation in our life and intentionally living from the heart reduces the suffering associated with the ego. As a mantra, the phrase 'I Am' immediately connects us to the Sun and strengthens the positive ego forces.

Sun Sign Astrology

In the birth chart, the Sun is our core self, yet also speaks of the male figures in our life, such as our father and other prominent males.

The whole idea of Sun-sign astrology is based on where our Sun is placed at birth and of course this sign is what makes us come alive and feel real. But it is not the full story by any means. All the twists and turns in our life story come about because of the way our other planets interact with our Sun. All of them take light from the Sun.

What follows is a guide to the meaning of the Sun's position in each sign, so that you can spot both its full light and shadow qualities. Here is the golden elixir carried by each Sun sign which shows us how to unlock our cosmic potential so that we can be who we came here to be.

Sun in Aries ♈

Element: Fire | Symbol: The Ram | Ruler: Mars

Aries Sunshine

You are born to be first – after all, you're the first sign of the zodiac and want to be a winner in life. This comes via competing with others, being super-quick at spotting the main chance and pushing yourself to be your personal best. Rams are naturally independent, sassy, go-getting and brave. You're a great initiator, so do best at start-up rather than follow-through. Your fiery Aries spirit requires a challenge that stretches your desire to conquer. Other people are inspired by your warmth and enthusiasm – your can-do philosophy is infectious.

Soul Superpower: Personal energy channelled into bold action.

Aries in the Shade

When the Sun isn't fully developed in Aries, you can turn your Mars-ruled heat and fire on others. You may seek to dominate other people to compensate for not being in your own centre of power. Constantly moving on to the next thing, leaving a trail of unfinished projects, is a sign of being essentially ungrounded. Alternatively, you never find courage. Then, meek as a lamb, you become disconnected from your sense of purpose.

Soul Evolution: Me-me-me is upgraded to bringing out the best in others.

Balancing the Aries Mind-Body-Spirit

Aries rules the head, which reflects your capacity to hold your head up high. The Aries life-force is essentially yang energy, clear and vital, which rises to the head. Aries is the typical hothead, both psychologically and physically – impulsive by nature and likely to produce fevers, migraines and inflammation when out of balance. As Mars, the planet of will, is your ruler, your wellbeing depends on being active, 'out there' and achieving. Mars has a symbolic connection with 'red blood' and you need to anchor free will into the blood and the very basis of your being. Therefore it's good for you to assert yourself. A healthy Aries needs plenty of scope to 'get on with it' and has a powerful connection to the spiritual world. If your self-esteem is low, your personal will downgrades to apathy, which is linked to depression. On the plus side, you have phenomenal vitality.

Health Hack: Do something!

Sun in Taurus ♉

Element: Earth | **Symbol:** The Bull | **Ruler:** Venus

Taurus Sunshine

The firm, steady energy of Taurus exudes reassurance and competence. Not easily diverted, you complete what you set out to do and your patience is legendary. You have an innate appreciation of the simple things in life and the practical ability of an Earth sign to manage, organize and remain grounded. Yet your special connection to Venus, the planet of beauty and love, gives you a poise that lends itself to manifesting your goals with ease.

Soul Superpower: Loyalty that promotes staying power and stability.

Taurus in the Shade

If you're unable to get in touch with your determination to 'make something of life', you tend to become obstinate, stubborn and stuck. Attachment to rigid attitudes prevents you from opening up to anything new. Your creativity dulls, your imagination freezes and you passively occupy space rather than actively welcome change.

Soul Evolution: Resistance to change is transformed into building something new.

Balancing the Taurus Mind-Body-Spirit

The Taurean affinity with Venus, goddess of love and affection, gives this Sun sign a luscious appeal. You're essentially comfortable in your own skin, and that makes others feel safe and relaxed in your company. Inhabiting your body with ease, you delight in all sensory pleasures. But whilst you thrive on the comforts and physical pleasures of life, too much indulgence can take a toll on your energy levels and wellbeing. Being tactile and understanding the healing properties of a hug is fundamental to your *joie de vivre*. Nature is also rejuvenating, healing and soothing for your soul. Taurus is associated with the neck and throat, and many Taureans have beautiful singing voices. Your weak spot can be the thyroid, and a sore throat or any stiffness in the neck is an early warning signal of imbalance in your system.

Health Hack: *Walk in nature.*

Sun in Gemini ♊

Element: Air | Symbol: The Twins | Ruler: Mercury

Gemini Sunshine

The playful, engaging quality of Gemini derives from a constant thirst for stimulation and diversity. Your naturally airy effervescence continually engages with life in a way that cross-pollinates ideas and connection. You are a collector of contacts and a multi-media hub of information. The twins' communication skills stem from the prowess of your ruling planet, Mercury, messenger of the gods, who is never on silent! Inquisitive, mobile and thriving on variety, Gemini is the social butterfly of the zodiac and a dazzling spin-master of concepts.

Soul Superpower: Versatility that creates channels for new ideas and inspiration.

Gemini in the Shade

Gemini's child-like quality, whilst enchanting, can become a default setting that keeps you unable to fully mature. If you aren't developing your adult sense of self, you avoid responsibility and become mentally scattered, fragmented and restless. You are unable to ground yourself and come across as being permanently distracted, always *en route* to somewhere else.

Soul Evolution: Commitment phobia is converted into a stimulating, evolving connection.

Balancing the Gemini Mind-Body-Spirit

The dualistic nature of the twins is easily split. Your words and deeds can be mesmerizingly agile or deceptively dangerous, as one twin denies the behaviour of the other. Adept at sleight-of-hand, you will find the most important element for your mental health is stillness. Cultivating presence, centredness and inner cohesion is the perfect antidote to your flighty, changeable nature and low boredom threshold. The parts of the body associated with Gemini are the lungs, arms and hands. Breathing is a big one for you, too – you can be a shallow breather or susceptible to lung weakness. The breath is the co-ordinator and collaborator between body and spirit, and, when flowing, can perfect the movement between inner and outer and stabilize the connection between body and spirit. This automatically calms the mind.

Health Hack: Be still and breathe deeply.

Sun in Cancer ♋

Element: Water | **Symbol:** The Crab | **Ruler:** The Moon

Cancer Sunshine

The watery realm of the lunar-ruled crab brims with emotional intelligence. You actively enjoy nurturing people, 'tuning in' to what's needed at any given time. Your intuitive sensitivity towards how other people are feeling enables you to respond with empathy. You have an affinity with the personal side of life, the inner realm, home, family and feelings. You create an emotional anchor for others and hold space for them.

Soul Superpower: Home is wherever you are.

Cancer in the Shade

If you get stuck in childhood patterns, you cling to the past with a level of attachment that prevents you from ever letting go. The crab as a creature can hold on with its pincer grip even if it's no longer alive! Dependency or co-dependency can be a thread that runs through relationships, with clinging and resentment disguised as suffering in the name of security.

Soul Evolution: Fear of abandonment is transformed into self-care.

Balancing the Cancer Mind-Body-Spirit

The crab has a tough outer shell that represents the boundary between the outside world and the soft inner self. Sensitive and self-protective, it switches between land and water, just as you switch between extrovert and introvert and need to be able to follow your own natural rhythms and moods. If undeveloped, you retain a paralyzing attachment to the past and are unable to individuate from your family of origin. Your wellbeing depends on being able to master your moods and touchiness. Cancer rules the breasts (mother's milk) and stomach, and the flow of mind-body-spirit is essential to keep these areas healthy.

Health Hack: Feed your soul with meaningful activities.

....

Sun in Leo ♌

Element: Fire | Symbol: The Lion | Ruler: The Sun

Leo Sunshine

A lover of life itself, the lion is a magnetic creature when he's in touch with his kingly qualities. With the Sun in Leo, you easily attract attention, inspire love, are a generous leader and radiate warmth with your sunny fire. Your style, creative flair and sheer magnificence light up the room, and indeed the world. Leo is ruled by the Sun and you can use solar power to shine and to bring out the best in others too. You have the capacity to turn something ordinary into pure gold.

Soul Superpower: Making people feel special through your heart energy.

Leo in the Shade

A lion whose ego is not in the heart is one cut off from love. Attention-seeking and self-centred around the little ego rather than the Higher

Self, locked into your own world-view, you adopt an arrogant attitude based on external showiness. Or, conversely, an imploded ego that doesn't rest in the heart. Never having received enough love to light up, you resent others and feel lost in life, without zest or purpose.

Soul Evolution: *Wounded ego becomes unconditional love.*

Balancing the Leo Mind-Body-Spirit

The heart isn't just a mechanical pump, but the seat of the spirit. It should be an organ of joy and a source of power for mind, body and spirit. Your radiance stems from a heart that is healthy in all its facets. If your heart feels numb, you can't fire on all cylinders. You need to know you're of true value and your gifts are well received. Lions who have dimmed their light can experience depression from lack of confidence. Yet emotional trauma can be repaired and the soul forces that live in the heart can restore you as the lion king. It's vital that you live from the heart and not as a caged lion. Your hero's journey involves an encounter with adversity to find your true identity, which in turn creates the authentic self.

Health Hack: *Spread the love with your big heart!*

Sun in Virgo ♍

Element: Earth | Symbol: The Virgin | Ruler: Mercury

Virgo Sunshine

The grounded Earth forces that flow through Virgo ensure that you know what's needed in any situation. As a worker bee, you pride yourself on keeping things running efficiently, often with a style of service that is close to devotion. Virgo is ruled by the mind planet, Mercury, which offers cleverness and discrimination, but your true gift is ensuring quality control, whilst your grip on reality provides excellent advice and support.

Soul Superpower: Acts of goodness that radiate healing.

Virgo in the Shade

If you haven't internalized your soul gifts, you can become prey to a nagging feeling of discontent and criticism that ruins any attempt at perfection. In the shade, you can either sacrifice yourself to others, becoming a workhorse, or wrap yourself ever more tightly in control that borders on OCD. Either way, in this mode, you feel that nothing is ever good enough.

Soul Evolution: Cynicism translates into making optimal choices.

Balancing the Virgo Mind-Body-Spirit

When you are in balance, you achieve a level of purity akin to a grain goddess, or perhaps your version of clean living, which makes you feel all is well in your world. You can either be a healer with the destiny to purify your relationship with Mother Earth or become contaminated by your sensitivity to pollution and impurities that are emotional, psychic and physical. Ultimately, correcting your own imbalances is key. Being self-effacing and non-assertive can prevent your ego from strengthening, eventually causing a non-filtration process in your psyche, and you can flip into addictive behaviour. If you can apply your fixing capacities to micro-managing all aspects of your wellbeing, you can experience optimum wellness.

Health Hack: *Zen to calm and centre yourself.*

Sun in Libra ♎

Element: Air | **Symbol:** The Scales | **Ruler:** Venus

Libra Sunshine

When the Sun is radiant in Libra, the air around you flows and you exhibit all the social skills and graces, whilst also being good at resolving differences and maintaining fairness. You see the whole as separate parts that need to be balanced and are involved in a continual process of adjustment that enables all sides to be seen and heard, appreciated and valued. You are cooperative and compromising in pursuit of the greater good and, as you are ruled by Venus, aesthetics, beauty and harmony are important to you.

Soul Superpower: *Relating in a way that enhances exchange and understanding.*

Libra in the Shade

If you never find that centred middle ground or inner knowing, you can be indecisive and betray your Self. If love is your drug, you can lose yourself in people-pleasing. Passivity is another issue – preferring to procrastinate or do nothing rather than create a stir. In the shade, your life remains in the shallow end of superficialities that neutralize the possibility of deep connection.

Soul Evolution: Needing to be liked becomes self-affirming presence.

Balancing the Libra Mind-Body-Spirit

Libra embodies the concept that no man is an island. Indeed, your whole sense of wellbeing depends on your relationship with other people and the wider world. As the sign of partnership, it's interesting that even your associated body part, the kidneys, naturally come as a pair! The kidneys monitor blood and reduce protein and sugar levels accordingly. This keeps the blood at peace. The kidneys and the adrenals that sit on top of them register fear and fright by releasing adrenaline, which creates the opposite of the harmony you seek. Harmony heals your bodily functions, blood pressure and wellbeing. Relationship issues tend to impact on your health, but when balanced, you are both grounded and centred in the body and open to the cosmos and spirit.

Health Hack: Find your still point at the centre.

Sun in Scorpio ♏

Element: Water | **Symbol:** The Scorpion | **Ruler:** Pluto

Scorpio Sunshine

The passion and intensity of Scorpio are such that they can be channelled into any activity, person or event that captivates your interest. At the highest level, you are a great healer and transformer of dark into light. In addition to the scorpion, there are three other symbols that are associated with Scorpio – the phoenix, the eagle and the dove. The phoenix rises from the ashes and is reborn, the eagle transcends and the dove finds peace after a storm. Your watery depths and inner strength penetrate what is hidden and your intuitive perception reveals the absolute truth.

Soul Superpower: Insight that delivers deep healing and transformation.

Scorpio in the Shade

All Scorpios have to go on a deep journey, usually triggered by crisis, which forces them to explore the psychological underworld. The arena in which they wrestle is beset with complexity over how much is given or taken in trust or betrayal. The poison pool of lower emotions and the sting in the tail are no places to hang out. But eventually you can surface from these experiences and transform them into soul wisdom.

Soul Evolution: Letting go with grace gives a surrender point of power.

Balancing the Scorpio Mind-Body-Spirit

The scorpion is an ancient creature, pre-dating dinosaurs, so it's no wonder your survival instinct is so strong! With Pluto as your ruling planet, you possess the capacity to come back from the brink and regenerate physically, emotionally and psychologically. Detoxing, eliminating and purging yourself of all that is negative is immensely healing for you. Your wellness depends on your capacity to see in the dark, refusing to encourage darkness and to integrate dark and light in yourself and your story. This sign rules the reproductive organs and the deepest form of soulful sexual union is also a means of healing.

Health Hack: *Detach from intense feelings.*

Sun in Sagittarius ♐

Element: Fire | **Symbol:** The Archer | **Ruler:** Jupiter

Sagittarius Sunshine

The archer or wise centaur inspires others with optimism. You're a motivator, teacher and way-shower, covering vast distances both mentally and geographically. Your fire spark is infused with good intentions and you move rapidly, always seeking to develop, grow and expand. Reaching out with warmth and playfulness and creating meaning in life, you are a positive force for good.

Soul Superpower: *Generosity and inherent kindness to others.*

Sagittarius in the Shade

Exuberant and excessively hedonistic, you are ungrounded and promise more than you can deliver. Always on the hunt for more, you can waste resources, scatter energies and chance your arm once too often. You live for the chase and the realm of potential and can't anchor yourself in the now. This reduces your destiny to a series of experiences you don't reflect on or learn from.

Soul Evolution: Taking things too far transitions into taking a wise, measured view.

Balancing the Sagittarian Mind-Body-Spirit

When out of balance, your centaur is focused on his wild animal nature in the realm of desire and needs to become the rider who can calm and guide his sacral fire. But your Sagittarian sense of humour and positive attitude plug you into the mains and enable you to move beyond setbacks with the minimum of damage. Sagittarius is ruled by Jupiter, the god of providence, and you can ride high on his benefic energy, although if you take it for granted, your self-indulgent streak will trip you up. The liver, hips and thighs are the areas associated with Sagittarius, and the liver in particular can become overloaded by unhealthy living.

Health Hack: Stop! Once in a while.

Sun in Capricorn ♑

Element: Earth | **Symbol:** The Goat | **Ruler:** Saturn

Capricorn Sunshine

The well-grounded goat is thought to be the earthiest of signs, on a mission to scale the material mountain. Yet the journey is actually a spiritual one and the climb turns out to go beyond the visible. The challenges you encounter in life are tests to develop your soul. Saturn's rulership of Capricorn provides the motivation to mature early and take on responsibility. You tend to carry a lot on your shoulders and wisely hold a great deal in reserve for the long haul. This instinctual knowledge of how to preserve and handle energy and resources is a great strength.

Soul Superpower: A sense of purpose that provides you with bearings in any situation.

Capricorn in the Shade

The practicality of Capricorn is accompanied by a pessimism that always sees the potential downside in any situation. Whilst this can be useful, it serves to darken your approach to life and creates a density that builds barriers to faith, optimism and even human intimacy. You can be ruthless in your climb, hard-heartedly rejecting anyone or anything that doesn't help you achieve your goal.

Soul Evolution: Tough love transitions into true love.

Balancing the Capricorn Mind-Body-Spirit

Capricorn's self-discipline is well documented, yet in ancient Rome the Saturnalia festival was held as a liberating antidote to obeying the rules. Being allowed to do anything you wanted during the festival was considered a necessary release that enabled society to function better. So, perhaps you would do well to include some frivolity and spontaneity in your careful lifestyle! Capricorn is associated with bones, skin and teeth – the scaffolding of the body – and it's hardly surprising that many Capricorns experience rigidity issues, tending to lighten up considerably in the second half of life.

Health Hack: *Relax.*

··

Sun in Aquarius ♒

Element: Air | **Symbol:** The Water-bearer | **Ruler:** Uranus

Aquarius Sunshine

The friendly water-bearer is way ahead of the game and synonymous with the Age of Aquarius, a new age of consciousness that is humanitarian rather than ego-based. Consequently, you can feel at odds with conventional society and prefer to do things your way, waking people up in the process. Born of the rational Air element, you find objectivity more comfortable than feelings. You can be an outsider, yet you have a knack of gathering people together. Free-spirited, you have an independent stance that appears radical to some, but contains the seeds of future living.

Soul Superpower: *Bringing people together to create a broader vision for change and intervention.*

Aquarius in the Shade

Having the wild planet Uranus as your ruler, you tend to act in a way that can come across as radical, disruptive or pushing boundaries. Your coolness can appear to be so detached, impersonal and cut off from feelings that it's hard for you to establish intimacy. Living only in the head is not conducive to true personal growth.

Soul Evolution: The lone ranger develops an independent soul connection.

Balancing the Aquarian Mind-Body-Spirit

The adrenaline surges of your ruling planet, Uranus, are quite tough on the nervous system – you live in a state of electrification, with its accompanying power surges and short-outs. The aim is to get your energy to flow steadily, so bringing any kind of regularity into your life helps to stabilize and earth you. You can become very distracted and mentally unavailable, even though connected to hordes of people. You are brilliant at dealing with the circuitry involved in groups of people and technology such as digital platforms and social media, but need to leverage your one-to-one relationships so as to create a balance and avoid personal alienation. Stepping into the heart is a way of making yourself fully present. The weak spots of the body most associated with Aquarius are the circulatory system and ankles.

Health Hack: Create a routine.

Sun in Pisces ♓

Element: Water | **Symbol:** Two fishes | **Ruler:** Neptune

Pisces Sunshine

The subtle watery realm and the Neptune rulership of Pisces point to the allure of great oceanic bliss, where ideals and the dream state merge and the starkness of material reality is mitigated. You float above it all with a transcendence that is otherworldly. You're a visionary, a highly intuitive soul who picks up far more than the ordinary five senses are able to scan. You *believe* – and that is a great gift that offers hope to those who have become more cynical. You also inspire others, creating special effects and layers of enchantment that lift the ordinary to the magical. Openness to the spiritual realm makes your life more soulful and luminous.

Soul Superpower: Magical, mystical attunement to creative Source energy.

Pisces in the Shade

The flip side of your vulnerability is the possibility of becoming a victim, a wounded soul who forgets how to heal. You can even escape from the real world and live a life of suffering and addiction, self-sabotage and avoidance that denies you the chance of gaining something solid, real and lasting. You would do well to use any lessons around loss as a means of learning discrimination.

Soul Evolution: Invisibility and lack of boundaries evolve into powerful inner co-ordinates.

Balancing the Pisces Mind-Body-Spirit

Pisces has an affinity with the immune and lymphatic system and the feet. Aside from the obvious need to ground yourself into the physical realm, you need to avoid making choices that allow your body and psyche to become receptacles for unwanted material. Instead, make them temples. Much hinges on actively engaging rather than passively accepting. You can be an extraordinary healer of the body, soul and mind, due to your unerring capacity to see what isn't immediately apparent or is even invisible. Yet your ability to access other realms must be balanced with a desire to calm any chaos in your own system and to establish a healthy relationship with all worlds.

Health Hack: Salute to the Sun.

CHAPTER 5

Moon

Emotional self, mother, yin, feminine energy, inner child, attachment, home, family, comfort zone

Where is my comfort zone?
What feeds my soul and fulfils my emotional needs?

Since time began, *La Luna* (☽ in your chart) has been an object of fascination, with her ever-changing but reassuring rhythm. She is the consort of the Sun and carries the deep inner feminine in relation to his outer-oriented masculine. Together they are known as the Luminaries and are the main *illuminators* of our chart. It is perfectly possible to capture the essence of a person simply by knowing their Sun and Moon signs. These show how their yin and yang are synthesized.

 The Moon presides over night and the unconscious, the Sun over day and the conscious.

Mother, Divine Mother, Inner Child

The sign our Moon is in shows us the celestial signature of our mother. Most importantly, how we experienced her nurturing and love. Was she there for us? What kind of emotional exchange did we have? Was her love conditional (if so, on what exactly), or unconditional? This early imprint becomes our love blueprint, because every time we bond with another human being it will bring up our early attachment and dependency issues.

At a soul level, the Moon is the great connection with divine mother energy. This alignment with the divine feminine takes place regardless of our gender or sexual orientation. When we're in flow here, we're not dissociated from our feelings. We can unlock what's inside us, relate to others, experience universal empathy and awareness, and access our intuition and innate capacity to commune with the intangible and unseen.

When we're open to our intuition, we can receive the gift of the sacred feminine – the deep inner knowing that isn't dominated by the rationale of the Sun.

The Moon is essentially regressive in nature, so we move into our Moon sign when we are tired and unconsciously return to our baby state, needy and less rational. The Moon is almost pre-verbal and non-verbal. Its language is emotional, intuitive, and expressed through feelings rather than words. Our Moon sign describes the emotional patterns we revert to when we are stressed and also those that underpin our need for security. These patterns create an unconscious emotional destiny unless we step into our choice-making potential.

In a nutshell, the Moon is our inner child.

The position of our Moon also highlights how safe we feel about being emotionally dependent on another person. Even what makes us feel safe.

The Moon is our retreat space, our sanctuary.

Yet there is also a hungry side to the Moon that needs to be fed with things, food-related and otherwise. So, how do we feed ourselves and with what? What do we look for to soothe us? What do we reach for to get into our comfort zone?

Home and Family

In some ways, the Moon is like an ingrained habit. It shows how we live and what makes us feel at home. We may not properly know someone until we see them at home, and relationships go to a new level when living together, because we are living with that person's Moon sign! Are you a neat-nick Moon in Virgo or a casual, laugh-a-minute Moon in Sagittarius? Sharing home space requires the blending of Moon signs.

But there is more... the Moon sign also shows the ancestors and shared memories that are handed down. So, the Moon is not to be trifled with. It's a summation of our lineage – our birth and soul family. We may not be able to change our past but we can cultivate conscious awareness, which helpfully reframes what we feel we've been born into so that we can understand the soul lessons we've chosen to experience. We can also create a soul family in this life-time which vibrates with the cosmic potential and comfort zone of our Moon.

Feelings

Above all, the Moon is the container of our feelings. We might have a watertight container in the form of Moon in Capricorn or something a lot more permeable, like Moon in Pisces. Our moods and emotions are expressed through our Moon sign. Since the physical Moon has an effect on fluids, there is a sense of fluctuation here too. We might be amped up – literally swollen up – at Full Moon, then withdrawn as our psychic and physical liquid is absorbed at New Moon.

The Moon's position by sign can make us either highly sensitized to the emotional realm and brimming with emotional intelligence or relatively cut off from our feelings and dominated by left-brain logic. Either way, we can often think that it's the outside world that needs changing, when really fulfilment is an inside job. We have to do the inner work and give ourselves the emotional healing necessary. It's only when we can nourish ourselves internally that we're really able to get the cosmic activation to transform our life.

If we feel empty on the inside, it can show up on the outside. Inner emptiness happens when we aren't in touch with our feelings, responses and inner realm, which translates as a kind of numbness and can cause others to wonder if there is 'anyone at home'.

To resolve this, we need to give ourselves permission to feel our feelings, rather than repress them. We have to care for ourselves. Our style of caring – for ourselves and others – is described by the Moon sign. Do we offer deep soulful care or light-hearted banter and distraction? Either way, when we are world-weary, in need of TLC, it is our Moon sign that holds us and sustains us.

Health and Healing

The kind of relationship we have with our body is suggested by our Moon placement. The body is a home or container for the spirit. But are we really at home in it, feeling safe and looked after? Where are we in terms of our capacity for bodily intimacy? Are we even in our body or do we take little notice of the physical realm and live in our thoughts?

The Moon is connected to bodily fluids such as blood, saliva, digestive enzymes and lymph and cellular fluid. It basically governs our moisture content. It is associated with the stomach, breasts, lymphatic system and digestion. It builds the brain. It is resonant with mother's milk and nutrition. Fluid holds memory and the Moon is associated with old, stuck memories.

Bloating, gut weakness, and ovulation are all connected to whether we have a healthy relationship with our Moon. But because it is a gentle, yin force, just being, listening and allowing things to be is a form of devotional healing. In this place of stillness and quietness, we can let go, accept and release what is blocked and locked in our tissues and cells.

When we receive the divine feminine energy that's inherent in our Moon, it becomes possible to energetically clear our body of old psychic residue.

Moon Phases and Effects

As seen from the Earth, the Moon is in a constant cycle of change as it orbits the planet, changing in size every night. These phases of the Moon form a predictable rhythm that has been seen since ancient times – a circular, cyclical story that unfolds through birth, death and rebirth over and over again, but continues to fascinate us.

We can acknowledge the phases of the Moon as divine timing. The ancient Egyptians recognized the Moon held the timing mechanism for planting cycles. It has an enormous gravitational pull on the tides, and the annual flooding of the Nile was the best time to plant crops. Nature is in harmony with the Moon's rhythm. Turtles and coral both time their fertilization with the Full Moon. River and sea tides go up at Full Moon and doctors report that surgery performed at that time results in additional bleeding. The body puffs up then and we can reset it at New Moon. The monthly female cycles are also similar in their timing to the lunar cycles.

Yet it's not just a physical frequency. Our moods are also pulled about according to the Moon's phases. Both our physical and emotional energy can fluctuate in synch with these cycles, especially if we're depleted or have a sensitive nervous system. But if we're feeling wiped out, in a yin-deficient state (we could call this a Moon-deficient state), new energy can be channelled down from infinite Source to revitalize us.

We are all born under a specific phase of the Moon, which reveals the interplay between the physical Sun and Moon, shedding light on whether our yin (Moon) and yang (Sun) energy flow together or are at odds. This gives us insight into the relationship between our mother (Moon) and father (Sun) too.

The two most dynamic Moon–Sun aspects in the chart are at New and Full Moon.

New Moon

This is the time of the grand alchemical union of Sun and Moon. Known as the conjunction, it is the fusion of yin and yang, and as such it carries great promise and potential.

 The New Moon marks the start of the new cycle and phase of life.

We are starting out in the dark, moonless night sky, which is a low-energy state. At this point it's important to cut the cords with what no longer serves us. A clean slate is needed to align with the full potential of the new cycle. Farming almanacs confirm this is a great time for planting, as the life-force is ready to be born in all of nature and begin its growth cycle in the dark. We can attune to the Moon cycles and ask a question at New Moon or start something new and receive the answer or a completion at Full Moon.

Born at New Moon

If you have the Sun and Moon conjunct – within 10 degrees of each other – then you were born at New Moon. The Sun and Moon may not necessarily be placed in the same sign if they are near the end or beginning of signs and their conjunction straddles both. If you are born at a New Moon, you will see in your chart's aspect table that your Sun and Moon are listed as being in conjunction (look for this glyph ♂).

If you are a New Moon person, you are infused with the birth energy of the Sun and Moon's union, which gathers tremendous force in one place. You could be described as a force of nature, a powerhouse of energy, an initiator. You adore harnessing the fresh energy of getting things moving. It can be more difficult for you to see another person's perspective, because the two most important celestial bodies are in the same place. This makes it a stretch of your bandwidth to align yourself with how another person thinks or feels. But this can help you self-actualize, as you don't need outside opinion or affirmation. Acting as a bridge between the past and the future is one of your gifts.

Full Moon

 The Full Moon is a portal of energy and opportunity and a punctuation mark for what has gone before.

It marks where the plot crescendos, where decisions, results and resolution come. It may even be an ending. So, it is a great time to tune in to what you're leaving behind. Sometimes at Full Moon the energy feels overwhelming, as emotions and responses are magnified, and what we haven't been aware of is brought into the light. If we didn't set an intention at New Moon, we may find that the Full Moon triggers unconscious or suppressed feelings, which can be revelatory. The celestial download can temporarily wipe us out or make us feel 'high' – witness the Full-Moon parties held in South East Asia. It's definitely a time when people go out – the roads are jammed, everywhere is busy.

Born at Full Moon

You are born at a Full Moon if the Moon is directly opposite your Sun at birth, within 10 degrees. Again, depending on whether your birthday is towards the beginning or end of the sign, the opposition might not occur in the exact opposite sign, but will be clearly marked on your chart's aspect table if you were born at a Full Moon (this glyph ☍ represents an opposition).

If you are a Full Moon person, you see beyond yourself. You easily connect with the 'otherness' in any situation. You recognize what someone else might want or need and relationships are often the catalyst for you to see yourself more clearly. The tension or pull between the celestial bodies, however, suggests reconciling opposing needs can be a challenge – perhaps your own split between head and heart, outer and inner, masculine and feminine. Or between you and another person. I have found my clients born on a Full Moon tend to experience their own parents as polar opposites.

Eclipses: The Big Before and After...

When either the Moon is between the Earth and the Sun (solar eclipse) or the Earth is between the Moon and the Sun (lunar eclipse), a big activation occurs.

> *Eclipses signify an energetic clearing as*
> *a result of a big celestial download.*

Universal energy pours into our body and affects every cell of our being. This can override our past conditioning, heal our core wounds, release old attachments and empower us to move into a new cycle. Whether it's a parting of the ways, an emotional crisis or a turning point, we always move towards greater light.

Lunar Eclipse (Eclipsed Full Moon)

It's eerie to see the Moon overcome by darkness and then return to light. But this can be a healing time. It is a time for laying an old struggle to rest. Sometimes circumstances force our hand. But we re-emerge. Eclipse energy can resonate for at least six months after the event.

Solar Eclipse (Eclipsed New Moon)

When the Sun goes dark, it is essentially a time of destiny, a time when we need to rise to a challenge. We receive new solar codes and transmissions and can develop greater intuition. The heightened energy can bring up unexpected desires, thoughts and events that have a prolonged effect, instigating a new beginning in our life.

Mapping the Moon Sign

 Our Moon sign is the most powerful soul signature of our emotional nature and inner life.

Find your Moon (☽) in your chart and read how it opens a door to your soul...

Moon in Aries ♈

It's really incredibly hard for you to sit back and relax, as you actually feel more comfortable when you're doing something! With this fiery Moon, you exude warmth and emotional courage through every pore. Other people are drawn to you when they need a fresh injection of energy. When their spirits are flagging or they've lost impetus, you always know exactly how to get them going again with a fresh surge of confidence.

You can't help showing how you feel, as the sign of Aries is spontaneous and impulsive, and add this to *La Luna* and you get a person who rushes in, responds at speed, acts first and thinks later. Your emotional nature is highly charged and you believe in being direct and upfront. There's something very immediate about you. Of course this makes you very engaging – people can't resist your warm energy and they feel they get to know you quickly. Your passion, enthusiasm and drive are infectious.

You're a great champion of those who don't or won't stand up for themselves, so fighting other people's corners comes naturally to you. It's possible you do this even if it isn't wanted! Taking it on is your default setting. Although you can lose interest in long drawn-out challenges, as you want a *result*.

At Home

Hard to live with? Dare I answer that question?! For those who prefer chilling, mooching, meditating and not doing anything very much, the answer is: 'Yes!' You're so active that sitting down for long is simply not your idea of fun. Arguments tend to flare up around you. Perhaps you provoke them by being so full-on. However, as you're not one to bear a grudge or sulk, the battle will be over as quickly as it began.

Comfort Zone: Doing what you love.
Pet Hate: Inertia.

Emotional Issue: Independence – how can you live your own life whilst being in a solid relationship?

....

Moon in Taurus ♉

The Moon is exalted in Taurus, meaning it shines most brightly in this sign. You're naturally drawn to the earthy and natural, whether it's the beauty of nature, scent or taste – well, you've got taste-buds that savour every single morsel! Tactile and affectionate, you find it easy to express yourself physically and you possess a strong and stable inner anchor that helps you keep steady emotionally.

Simplicity is your mantra. You have a knack of being able to soothe others with a hug or a cup of tea. Other people recognize that you're dependable, loyal and not given to emotional outbursts or flighty behaviour. You value emotional security and can weather many storms simply by staying put and allowing them to blow over.

You tend to take things literally, not looking beyond the visible or reasonable and therefore not overreacting, and it can be hard for you to understand why others may do so.

Your practical outlook helps you through life and you like to take your time and plan things out rather than playing them by ear. Common sense is one of your strengths, enabling you to cut through the unnecessary elements and find a solution to a problem without getting caught up in it.

At Home

Being a rock is your default setting. Your attachment style is basically secure and security-driven. You dislike change and form bonds that are built to last. You enjoy keeping the home running smoothly as a container for your creature comforts. You adore pampering yourself – and others, as you need your special tokens of abundance to be freely available.

Comfort Zone: Cashmere and fine foods, sex and shopping.
Pet Hate: Sudden change.
Emotional Issue: Money – when do you have enough? The accumulator in you hangs on to everything.

....

Moon in Gemini ♊

Like quicksilver, you flit around the realm of feelings and emotional attachment – sometimes in, sometimes out. It can be hard to pin you down, as you like to be in constant motion, switching your responses, reactions and location in an instant. People find you amusing and interesting, as you always have something to say. Verbal exchange is your means of maintaining connection. It means you come from your head more easily than your heart.

Your rational approach to life tends to make light of feelings. You don't want to get swamped in emotions, so tend to reason your way around the essentially non-rational mood swings and responses of others. It buys you some room to breathe, but others can find your unwillingness to 'go there' rather superficial.

Your great gifts are connecting people and keeping things moving. A natural curiosity about life keeps you constantly updated, and you can be something of a news junkie too. You like to feed your mind with a variety of stimulants and you're a brilliant mixer of people, enjoying the cocktail of different viewpoints. Of course, this also means you have a low boredom threshold, so those close to you have to keep you on your toes!

At Home

You may actually have two homes, which satisfies your dualistic nature. Even in a single dwelling, you have people constantly coming and going, so those who actually live with you find the home more of an open house than a sanctuary. But your restless spirit needs new people to provide a breath of fresh air.

Comfort Zone: Newsfeed.
Pet Hate: Repetition.
Emotional Issue: Can you ever settle down or settle in?

Moon in Cancer ♋

With the Moon in the sign of the crab, you're very protective of those you love – and can be self-defensive too, yet totally warm and mushy on the inside. No other sign nurtures others like Cancer, and having the Moon there offers you rich emotional intelligence. You long for emotional connection, bonding and union. Of course, being ruled by the ever-changeable Moon means there are many fluctuations in your moods and feelings.

You know how to make people feel at home, both in your company and where you live. You emit a vibration of home so that people instinctively seek out your place as one they can instantly relax in and draw comfort from. You have an instinctive capacity to read what others need at any given time. You simply tune in to people with your phenomenal emotional antennae and capacity to summon up the exact support, insight, or empathic response required.

Your attachment style is quite clingy – once your pincers are in, some people may struggle to get free. Yet those who appreciate your emotionally nourishing energy would never be able to replicate it elsewhere. Cancer is ruled by the Moon, the foremost symbol of the Great Mother or divine mother, and you literally channel its nurturing energy.

At Home
You long for domestic bliss and the ideal home. Your place is stuffed with comforting memories, antiquities or heirlooms, even transitional objects! You're vintage-oriented and create a home, not a minimalist 'space'. Living with you is personally rejuvenating for those who want to be doted on. Yet the crab can also be crabby – your super-sensitive feelings propel you into taking everything personally.

Comfort Zone: Tea and sympathy.
Pet Hate: Cold hearts.
Emotional Issue: Abandonment – how could you/would you?

Moon in Leo ♌

As you would expect with the Moon in the grand and showy sign of Leo, your personal life might verge on the dramatic or the upscale! You would never do anything by halves and want to be worshipped and adored, whilst also radiating a warmth of spirit that makes those in your orbit feel special. You have a great flair for creating a show-home, or at the very least making the best of whatever you've got.

You create sparkle and shine, even if you can't resist dominating the proceedings! You are the very centre of the home and family – the one around whom the others revolve. Yet you possess a playful creativity that negates your occasionally high-handed manner, and you can give others the star treatment. You light up the room with your love of life, so nothing is ever dull around you.

Being taken for granted would be the killer for you. You prefer to be put on a pedestal; at the very least you must receive appreciation for all that you give to others. A little recognition ensures you remain the pussy cat rather than the prima donna. No one would want to risk the lion's roar of disapproval.

At Home
You are always front of house, never the slave or the backroom person. Those who enter your palace are treated to every luxury. You can throw a tantrum, but your charisma is never compromised for long. Basically, you just want to love and be loved, but you must never forget the simple things speak just as well as the bling!

Comfort Zone: The best of everything.
Pet Hate: Lacklustre energy.
Emotional Issue: Feeling entitled to special treatment.

....

Moon in Virgo ♍

The fastidious nature of Virgo makes the Moon in this sign naturally fussy and acutely critical of imperfections. This can be wonderful if you're a curator, or work in the health, hygiene or standards sector. Wherever you are, your gift for organization is useful in ensuring everything is working perfectly.

Virgo is an Earth sign, so your natural affinity with Mother Nature and the body has a healing quality. You understand the workings of the natural cycles, the ingredients of the Earth and the intricacy of the body.

Virgo is a busy bee, so with the Moon here, you like to be useful to others. You respect the idea of service and helpfulness, which is the antitheses of the ego and accolades. In fact, you can be selfless when it comes to giving to others. You run around performing all those little tasks that make the world, or the home, go round.

Yet your attachment style can be quite anxious. Emotions aren't your thing; you much prefer rationalizing and analyzing what's going on. Your capacity for discernment is high, which can make you perfectionist and judgemental, but you dislike any form of emotional self-indulgence. Others are drawn to your impeccable quality control and your gentle, discreet, well-ordered responses. That is when you're not worrying about the probability of things going wrong, which for you seems to be very high.

At Home

Who wouldn't want to live in a perfectly run environment? Your efficiency is a wonder to behold. In fact, you never run out of anything! However, there can be a lack of spontaneity, an inability to let things be, certainly to relax, which makes you 'difficult to live with'. Things are never quite right for you. 'Could do better' is your mantra. Yet there won't be a thing out of place.

Comfort Zone: Clean living.
Pet Hate: Untidiness.
Emotional Issue: Not feeling good enough.

Moon in Libra ♎

If you have *La Luna* placed in the loved-up sign of Libra, relationships are always going to be your emotional base-point. You seek harmony, beauty and equilibrium, and therefore dislike any kind of negativity, imbalance, quarrelling or ugliness. This makes you very easy to be with. Yet it's not always easy for you – you're always adjusting the scales to accommodate the other person.

The world of appearances is very important to you, which makes you keen to present yourself well, and you want those close to you to cooperate in making things look good. In your idealistic world, everyone is polite and perfectly formed. Yet, as you can only see yourself in relation to another, this in itself creates a disparity, as others might not be aware of what you really need. And you're the keeper of the peace, so you zip up your own feelings in order to maintain it.

However, your gift for compliance and negotiation does take the heat out of any differences of opinion. You smooth things over, even if you find yourself caught in the middle of other people's *contretemps*. You can procrastinate, though, and go along with something for fear of upsetting others, and your indecisive nature can produce problems in the long run. You're so attached to the idea of a perfect relationship it can be hard to live with faults, or even to choose someone to be with!

At Home
A beautiful home is super-important to you. Yours will be a bastion of good taste and colour coordination. In it, you practise the graceful art of relationships and you prefer others to set the pace whilst you revolve around them, but this comes at a price if your own feelings never get a look-in.

Comfort Zone: Good-looking people in an ideal home.
Pet Hate: Rudeness.
Emotional Issue: People-pleasing.

Moon in Scorpio ♏

Quite simply, you are similar to Loch Ness: on the surface all seems calm, but a monster may lurk underneath! No stranger to the darker nuances of the emotional realm, you are fascinated by feelings that others may not want to know about, still less experience. It's all part of the Scorpionic passion and intensity. For you, highs and lows, light and dark, must have equal billing and be part of your journey to emotional honesty and authenticity.

You have a penetrating ability to see deep inside other people, too, and nothing difficult puts you off. This is why people are either magnetized to you or a little scared of you – because you are the one person who 'gets it'. You become deeply attached to others and can be possessive and difficult to handle when you reach the extremes of your emotions. Yet for the most part your feelings are private, hidden away. Your inner world is rich!

Your complex nature comes across as either all-encompassing or simply not interested. You can stir things up with your insatiable desires and wound with your cutting remarks – your Scorpionic sting. You have a Pandora's Box of secrets to unveil, deliciously slowly.

At Home

The 'Do Not Disturb' sign is permanently on your front door, as you like to live privately, allowing only a trusted few into your inner sanctum. But you are fiercely loyal to those you love. As for your home, there won't be anything ordinary about it. It will be full of exotic pieces, deep colours and curious items that tell a story. The Ikea mentality is not yours! For you, home is where magic happens.

Comfort Zone: Home alone.

Pet Hate: Shallowness.

Emotional Issue: Whom can you trust?

....

Moon in Sagittarius ♐

Domestic duties, familial obligations, ties that bind – none of these sit easily with the Moon in the free-spirited sign of Sagittarius. It's not that you won't settle down. You will, but in your own style and with your own set of values and needs. As the archer is the explorer, you may even find that your spiritual home is somewhere quite different from where you landed at birth. Even another country!

You're emotionally generous, fun to be around, playful and uplifting – these qualities are your main draw. There's a warmth about you, and a spontaneity that is life-enhancing for others. You're not one to let the grass grow under your feet. You like to be active, doing or learning something. In some ways, you are a traveller who sees home as simply somewhere to rest before the next adventure.

Your attachment style can be quite loose. For a start, it's hard to keep up with you or pin you down to a commitment. Your sense of fun and joking nature are infectious, yet the deeper nuances of emotional connection may not apply. Your criteria for bonding are whether you can have a good time with someone, feel relaxed with them and discuss your philosophy of life.

At Home

You're searching for something that is unlikely to be found at home. You're a seeker rather than a stay-at-home. You prefer to live in a casual and relaxed way, without too much routine to snare you. The family need to give you space! Plus you love the great outdoors and being in nature. Small buildings aren't your thing!

Comfort Zone: Camping out, festivals, parties.
Pet Hate: Expectations.
Emotional Issue: Staying in one place.

....

Moon in Capricorn ♑

The Moon in the most responsible sign of the zodiac confers an air of maturity and control, which means you're always aware of the bottom line in any personal situation. It's hard for you to give spontaneous expression to how you feel. You don't want to come across as vulnerable, so you contain your feelings, sit on them, repress them or even deny them.

However, when it comes to being there for people, it is you who provides the shoulder to cry on. You have a rock-like capacity to withstand emotional storms, both yours and other people's, so it's not much wonder they turn to you when in need of a tower of strength. However, it's not sympathy that you offer, but practical help and a somewhat wry but nonetheless consoling understanding of how life can go pear-shaped at times!

Emotionally, you can be a tough nut to crack. You don't give in to your own feelings or want to rely on other people. You're all about self-sufficiency, even survival, so you're the coper, not the needy one. As a child, you were older than your years, so you may never have had the chance to be as irresponsible or playful as some of the other Moon signs. Yet you have a dry sense of humour and you relax in later life.

At Home
You like to feel safe and secure, so you're attracted to places that have a holding, containing feeling. You can live alone quite happily or head up a family. Whichever way, you organize everything and make sure it works. You're a realist rather than a romantic, sometimes withholding your feelings and living as if you are hermetically sealed. You can seem cold, hard and impenetrable to those who wear their heart on their sleeve.

Comfort Zone: Classic.
Pet Hate: Silliness.
Emotional Issue: Repressing and controlling your feelings.

Moon in Aquarius ♒

Friendship forms the hub of your personal life. It's not that family isn't important, but you love to be part of a group of non-blood-related people. You get flashes of precognition and adore spontaneity, but don't like to be engulfed by emotions. Detachment and rationality come naturally to you, allowing you to step back from dramas. This cool approach is healing balm to those who can't get distance on how they feel.

Open and friendly, you gather friends and followers easily, and you love to mix it up, so your tribe is diverse and non-denominational! Your vibe is electric and independent. You have your own stance and you instinctively want to explore the unusual or extraordinary. The freedom to do your own thing is important.

Altogether, you can offer a different perspective on life, along with some objectivity and inspiration. You have the ability to magic something up that takes others by surprise.

At Home
You're not particularly attached to the way things *ought to* or *should* be around the home, which makes for an eclectic environment with your own personal style. Sociability is key, so your doors are open to others, but you're equally happy alone.

Your Comfort Zone: Chilling with friends.
Your Pet Hate: Narcissists.
Emotional Issue: Detaching from your feelings.

Moon in Pisces ♓

You are essentially sensitive and dreamy, soulful and empathic. You totally get where another person is coming from. You can read their aura, their mood and everything that's floating in the atmosphere, whether you want to or not.

It can be hard to have boundaries when you're so connected to the emotional quantum field. Besides, your sixth sense tells you when something is going on, so it's impossible to 'not know'. You're a person who gives a lot, who has a lot of compassion for others, yet you can be impressionable and easily influenced, or even ungrounded if you aren't able to connect to the inner you.

A romantic idealist, you long for others to be their best selves and can give people too many chances and experience disappointment and loss as a result. However, on the upside, you can transcend all the dross in life and reach the heights of bliss. In terms of attachment, you can be either avoidant or co-dependent!

At Home
You naturally go with the flow and are able to adapt to people and places very well. Your home is often a retreat or sanctuary, your special bubble, with mood lighting, music and ambient effects. You absorb other people's feelings and are super-responsive to their needs, which can maintain harmony but sometimes lead to being overwhelmed.

Comfort Zone: Sleeping and dreaming.
Pet Hate: Reality!
Your issue: Fear of abandonment.

CHAPTER 6

Mercury

*Thinking, learning, communicating,
engaging with others*

What is my message?
What is my communication style?
Why is my perspective important?

Mercury (☿ in your chart) is the planet of the mind – how we think, learn, communicate.

 **Mercury is our mental state and outlook;
it's what we notice, and therefore our
reality is formed through its filter.**

Mercury has a message and perspective to give to the world. Its element gives an initial clue as to what this is: a Fire sign Mercury (Aries, Leo, Sagittarius) jumps at a new idea; an Earth sign one (Taurus, Virgo, Capricorn) offers grounding and practical thinking; an Air sign Mercury (Gemini, Libra, Aquarius) connects ideas and spreads the word with logic and objectivity; and a Water sign one (Cancer, Scorpio, Pisces) is intuitive and conveys a personal message.

In essence, Mercury reveals the power of our mind, and its position will also show the kind of relationship we have with multimedia and digital platforms. In addition, Mercury is associated with all our comings and goings, motion and movements, especially short journeys, education and siblings. It presides over buying and selling, negotiating, trade and transactions.

 Mercury is the connector, the go-between
for the internal and external realms.

Its activity is similar to the in- and out-breath and it is ruled by Gemini, the quintessential mercurial Air sign, and Virgo, and is connected to the lungs.

Always On

There's no doubt that the speed at which messages can be sent over vast distances nowadays is something even Hermes, messenger of the gods, may never have envisaged! He was the only god with access to all areas, including the heights of Mount Olympus and the underworld, mirroring the way our own thoughts can take us high or low.

What technology has presented us with now is the capacity to make news, thoughts and ideas available 24/7. But, although we are more connected than ever before, the price we pay for speed is a loss of time to reflect. Our nervous systems are constantly bombarded by Mercury's messages – we are always 'on', always being updated, whether through newsfeed, business emails or personal messages. In the age of multimedia platforms, we exist on a diet of snippets and fragments, and our thinking can become de-personalized and skewed by other people's thought forms. It's no surprise that Mercury is the planet connected to *mental health*.

The first thing we need to do is become aware of our own thoughts and perspective. To get hold of our own truth.

Connected or Disconnected?

Everyone can be contacted now, but is that true communication? If thoughts have wings, in the form of either Hermes or WhatsApp, then we are being shown that the capacity to speak to or message one another doesn't mean we feel energetically connected. We're always in a hurry and don't take time to truly understand something and think it through – and we are expected to respond immediately! It is one of the greatest paradoxes of this so-called Age of Connection that many of us feel more isolated and lonely than ever before. It seems the mind alone cannot meet our need for true human exchange. Meaningful connection only happens when Mercury connects with the heart.

Zen Mind or Wild Horses?

It's so easy to identify with our mind, to get into the wild horses/ runaway horse syndrome where our thoughts control us, instead of the other way around. The Zen mind, on the other hand, is pure bliss, emptiness, clarity – how can we get there even if we aren't meditating?

First, we need to remember that the mind isn't everything. We're not our scrambling thoughts, opinions or memories. We give them so much airtime, and the brain is incredible, but the heart brain or the gut instinct might be closer to the truth. Steadying our mind to reveal our own inner truth is important – perhaps more important than ever before. The brain tends to be revered as being of primary significance in defining and coordinating all our thoughts and activities. On one level this is true, but the brain is not the true centre of consciousness in spiritual terms. That's the heart.

Our Own Thoughts?

If we think of Mercury as a kind of scanner that picks up signals from the outside world, with all its news stories, emails, conversations and exchanges, we get an idea of how impactful the small planet Mercury is in our daily lives.

 Mercury is the channel through which we connect with other people and the world. By taking control of our thoughts, we can take control of our destiny.

Yet in a world of information overload, readily available comments and 'influencers', our thoughts can get blurred and enmeshed with other people's very easily. Can we even be sure that we are really thinking our own thoughts? Are we absorbing someone else's instead?

Also, part of Mercury's job is to express who we are. Perhaps we do have our own ideas, but are we able to voice them?

Our personal Mercury will give us clues to all these things and who we really came here to be.

What's Trending?

We all have our own personal newsfeed of repetitive thoughts and stories. We experience our own thoughts trending, find it hard to take our mind off certain things and get distracted by thoughts that come in seemingly randomly. Our constant internal chatter can distract and distort our perception.

 What is trending in our own newsroom is deeply connected to how we perceive and align ourselves with the world.

It's almost as if our brain has cookies deposited in it that mark and trace our associations and connections.

We operate within the quantum field, the psychic field of all life, and can get contaminated and hooked in unless we consciously step out of it from time to time. Fortunately, developing a higher level of awareness enables us to become an editor and decide what we want to think about.

Mercury on the Dark Side

The physicist Brian Cox describes the planet Mercury as a 'small and tortured world'. Indeed, its polar regions never see light, contrasting with its hot spots to create the greatest extremes in temperature of any planet in the solar system. We can see Mercury's connection with the dark areas of communication in the form of spin, gossip, news-trash, trolling, buried and fake news, deceit, online bullying, remote viewing and 'bad' news.

News stories that are laced with drama and toxicity feed us fear, which is a media favourite that hooks us in. The more we are triggered and click into this media-generated news, the more frequently we retrace the *fear-based neural pathways in our brain*, which in turn meshes us with the fear that lurks in the collective unconscious.

Allowing our mind to be infiltrated in this way can lead to our conscious mind being overridden. Thoughts can be actually thoughtless, i.e. without consciousness. We become mindless rather than mindful. Opinions can be hugely biased and based on assumptions or projections rather than truth. If we are overwhelmed by what other people think, we can lose the capacity to question and connect to what's true for us.

So it's important to realize that Mercury is a double agent. Hermes can zoom into our lower unconscious, connecting the dots and interpreting a news story in a way that lowers our vibration, but he can also fly high and connect us to wisdom. He is a good symbol for Gemini's duality, as he is both thief and magician.

 Hermes/Mercury moves us between dark and light.

Our mind can be filled with obsolete data, too, but old memories or repetitive thoughts can be released, freeing us from the entrapment and stagnation of the past.

Transformational Mercury

Choosing to let go of thoughts that keep us stuck can be a real step forward in life. So, Mercury can be a gateway to greater freedom, happiness and peace of mind. This is different from being either more left- or right-brained; it is to do with living from our infinite soul mind instead of inside our ego-based mind. We can make space to observe and accept without judgement. But can we live from a place of clarity and choice?

***The good news: if we think of our mind
as being like software, then we can consciously
upgrade it, remove psychic viruses
and reboot our entire system.***

Mercury's power for good is immense: it can be a revelatory force that turns our own transformational journey into a message that can be relayed to help others. It can also be the conduit to a totally new understanding of ourselves, others and what life is about. To reach that new understanding, we need to stop kidding ourselves, telling ourselves the same old stories, and make a change that takes us out of the past. We have to work at cultivating clarity and becoming intuitively clear.

Take a look at your frequent messaging and evaluate whether it is negatively impacting your clarity of mind. The monkey mind that has us darting about, watching a screen, texting a message and holding a conversation, is not centred and focused enough to pay attention to the words. What kind of white noise and chatter do you have going on at any one time?

If what you're thinking isn't serving you, you can develop a different relationship to it.

> *The simplest instant meditation is to close your eyes, take some deep breaths and release everything that came before this moment!*

From a Soul Perspective: Moving from Ego Thinking (the Small Mind) to Soul Thinking (Wisdom)

The mind has such a hold on us. We identify with it to such a degree that we believe what we think is true. Yet what we are experiencing is filtered through our ego mind. It's not the experiences themselves that cause the problem, but the way we think about them. If we truly want to experience big shifts in our life, we need to get out of our comfort zone and begin to look at things differently.

> *Mercury is the planet that can take us from one state to another quick as a flash.*

Whatever our old way of thinking, it's always possible to have a radical transformation if we can interrupt the old story we tell ourselves and rewrite the script.

The healing power of the mind is the greatest medicine. We are at a crucial shift in perspective now in terms of what we think and believe. Limited, materialistic thinking, and even information itself, are not of the higher mind. Awareness, meaning and understanding are the entry points into the super-conscious mind.

Hermes is our guide and on tap 24/7 to transport us from hell to heaven, from unconscious to superconscious, if we are open to seeing things differently.

 Changing our thoughts changes our life!

A Few Words about ... Mercury Retrograde!

Three times a year Mercury appears to travel backwards – goes into retrograde – in the heavens for a period of approximately three and a half weeks, coinciding with a period of mayhem. The planet doesn't really turn retrograde; this is an optical illusion as viewed from Earth.

Remember Mercury has a trickster energy. In retrograde motion, he can be the unseen force that trips us up. When Mercury goes retrograde, we can experience:

* 'slow mo'
* bad reception
* slip-ups
* disorganization
* stops and starts
* lost and found
* u-turns
* revisions and changes
* connections with the past
* trick or treat
* mixed messages

- messages not getting across
- things getting lost, or lost in translation
- people not listening to us or receiving what we have to say
- travel being delayed
- plans collapsing
- communications breaking down
- equipment and technology failing

Who hasn't had the urge to blame their problems on Mercury retrograde?! But, despite our irritation at everything being on a go-slow or our best-laid plans changing, the process of Mercury retrograde is divinely inspired to get a message to us. We have to be interrupted in our daily life in order to hear that message. We are thrown out of kilter so that we can receive it. This can feel like an intervention, but if we go beyond the frustration of our journey being interrupted or our computer crashing, we'll find we're being given some space and time to look into what's really going on.

A real epiphany can take place when the Sun joins Mercury halfway through the cycle. This is the 'Aha!' point and it can feel as if we now understand why we have reached a sticking point or must move away from an old activity or pattern of behaviour. Mercury retrograde is actually a catalyst for *awareness*. Out of the unknown, the void, the space, comes new insight. If we examine where we're going and what's happened, we get the gold: a moment of truth, realization, recognition. We receive the missing piece of the jigsaw.

So many positives can come out of Mercury retrograde if we view it as a natural cycle of punctuation, a necessary break in the proceedings in order to retrieve vital information. We have to learn to be patient and use this time for planning, reviewing, fixing, thinking and strategizing about what we want to do when we can step forward again.

Mercury Information

Our Mercury sign shows how we connect and engage with others, how we think and learn, what we've got to say and how we say it.

So, how does *your* Mercury work? Look at the sign of your Mercury to see the specific ways in which you perceive and receive, process and communicate thoughts and information.

Mercury in Aries ♈

With Mercury in Aries, you are quick on the uptake and in a rush to get the gist of what others are saying and put your own message across. If people take too long to explain something to you, they will be given short shrift! It's all about getting to the point with no fluff. This is because you get no satisfaction from listening to something unless you can *do* something about it. You are almost impatiently tapping your feet, muttering, 'Next, next,' and your desire to intervene isn't restrained very often!

On the plus side, you're enthusiastic about ideas and able to galvanize others into following suit. Whilst people may feel rushed along in your company, they will always turn to you for a direct and honest opinion. You've a gift for speaking up with confidence and daring to say what you think. You can be strongly idealistic and, being the first to spot something, a driving force. As an initiator, you eagerly pursue many strands and projects, as your mind easily embraces concepts and ideas. The problems begin with the follow-through – you are best off delegating that to those who enjoy the practical, mundane details.

Soul Gift: Rapid transmission.
Unlocking Your Cosmic Potential: Actively cultivating patience grounds your thinking.

Mercury in Taurus ♉

Your methodical mind likes time to consider and digest all the material available rather than thinking on the spot. You aren't one to make up your mind about something without giving it your full thought. When you do give advice, you'll have done the due diligence first and therefore your words will be of high practical value rather than plucked out of the air. You value the tried and tested, and ideas that have worked in the past. You dislike plans changing or not having a schedule, as you always prefer to be on solid ground and get discombobulated without a structure.

Being reliable has its rewards, as others depend on your unflagging aptitude. A bit like the tortoise who wins the race, you will see something through to the end, no matter what it takes. If those that rush in tend to view you as slow and steady, you are still perfectly happy to do things at your own pace and develop a routine and rhythm that outlasts all the chancers that drop out at the merest hint of challenge. Not given to huge flights of fancy, you are clever at spotting what is valuable and viable and has a natural affinity with the material realm of life. Your perspective is earthy and grounded, and you value what is workable.

Soul Gift: Perseverance.
Unlocking Your Cosmic Potential: Opening your capacity to embrace the new, whilst remaining calm and steady, gives you a more rounded perspective.

....

Mercury in Gemini ♊

Gemini is ruled by Mercury and therefore works to its best advantage here in terms of dazzling wordplay and expression. Many media types and communications people have Mercury here. With this placement, your natural way with words is immediately apparent. Of course, getting enough stimulation into your constantly hungry mind is an issue, which is why you tend to listen to and watch several things at once. Your mind can assimilate fragments and spin them together, and the monkey mind is always 'on', allowing little rest from thoughts and dialogue. You tend towards a huge identification with the mind – from your perspective, everything can be calculated and measured through thought – but this can block access to the heart.

At one with digital media and social networking platforms, you're rarely incommunicado. Your multitasking capacity is enormous and you're very capable of operating more than one business simultaneously. You just love to engage with people and cross-fertilize information and opinions. To some, you come across as the fount of all knowledge; to others, as a lightweight who flits across the surface of things. Verbiage is your inexhaustible resource, whilst the duality of the twins means your constantly moving dialogue may be your absolute truth or merely an *en passant* observation. Either way, your wit and repartee distract people from any inaccuracy!

Soul Gift: Cleverness.

Unlocking Your Cosmic Potential: Finding a still point of focus protects you from chasing too many ideas and allows you to develop greater intuition.

....

Mercury in Cancer ♋

The neural pathways of this Mercury are almost sponge-like! You have an incredible capacity to soak up impressions, information and memories. They enter your being and pass through your very personal perspective before being deposited in your storage system. In fact, you hold on to thought forms like no other sign. You can recall things from long ago that no one else can remember, partly because you file them with a unique emotional memory code that enables you to access them with ease. Your memory bank extends way beyond logic.

Intuition is your secret weapon. Your emotional antennae are permanently switched on, so you sense and intuit the non-verbal as much as the verbal. Your gut feeling is a brain in itself, which feeds your impressions and intuition. This means your opinions are coloured by what you feel, yet you remain uncannily accurate in your observation of what's going on, including picking up the subtle clues that most people miss. You know how to engage with others and reel them in with the stories you tell. This has its advantages, yet more left-brained people may unnerve you with their no-frills approach.

Soul Gift: Understanding.
Unlocking Your Cosmic Potential: Actively cultivating impartiality gives you distance, clarity and breathing space from your personal perceptions.

Mercury in Leo ♌

You are a royal personage rather than a messenger, which imbues your words with great impact. This has pluses and minuses, as you can either enthral others with your voice of authority or repel them with your sense of entitlement. Whilst there are occasions for leading with your opinions, there can be times when it's best to dial it down a bit and listen to the voice of the people! However, you do have a knack for conveying your thoughts with the Fire sign energy of positive enthusiasm. From your perspective, *your* point of view counts, and it's therefore important to think for yourself.

Learning from others involves humility, and you have a certain amount of pride, which can translate into thinking you know best. You prefer to be in charge, mentally at least! Yet you know how to lead and make decisions with conviction. The flip side of this is your belief that you're never wrong! But give you an audience and you come into your own, whether in a Zoom meeting or on a stage, holding everyone spellbound with your dramatic flair.

Soul Gift: Talking with confidence.
Unlocking Your Cosmic Potential: Making space to really hear what others are saying engages you with them more deeply.

....

Mercury in Virgo ♍

You are the wordsmith, finding the precise descriptions for everything, all perfectly punctuated of course! Ruled by Mercury, you are the more down-to-earth sibling of Gemini. Accuracy matters to you, as do careful timing and delivery. Therefore you are unlikely to speak out of turn or make blunders. Perhaps you can be overly attached to small details that others overlook, which can be infuriating to them. However, if you engage with work where these things count, then you are in your element.

You speak gently and quietly, yet your opinions are thoughtful and well considered, therefore much in demand. You spot the flaw in the argument and the fly in the ointment, and this can be very useful. Brilliant with the small print and contractual matters, you have a level-headed approach and can be relied upon to produce excellent work to the best of your ability. You have a talent for analyzing, contrasting and perfecting. Although you can be critical, fussy and hard to please, you have such high standards you can be rather critical of yourself. Anxiety is a product of a mind that rarely switches off. But you have the ability to see what's behind every view or event and the process that led up to it.

Soul Gift: Observation.
Unlocking Your Cosmic Potential: Allowing things to be as they are without judgement produces a state of inner calm and acceptance.

....

Mercury in Libra ♎

The finesse of Mercury in Libra produces beautiful words, diplomacy and strategy. You are someone who likes to engage with contrasting ideas without engaging in combat. You can sugarcoat even the worst news and neutralize warring factions by focusing on the one thing that everyone agrees with. Brilliant at negotiating, or presenting information in a pleasing way, you disarm people with your charm. You have a reputation for saying exactly the right thing to please others. Being polished in your presentation is your great asset.

Allowing others to lead the way, you can make them think that what you want all along is actually their idea! Seemingly impartial and appearing indecisive, you nonetheless operate in a way that compares all options and weighs them up before commitment. You're able to make people see another side of an argument in a non-threatening way. However, as you dance between both ends of the scale, others may find it difficult to know what you really believe.

Soul Gift: Fairness.
Unlocking Your Cosmic Potential: Applying the principle of fairness to your interactions with others enables you to assert and speak your truth as well as receive their views.

Mercury in Scorpio ♏

Nothing superficial here – your powers of perception penetrate to the heart of the matter. Performing a psychic X-ray on everyone and everything, you see all of the unconscious, hidden, psychological, subtle angles, whilst others deal with what's available on the surface. Being a private investigator (with or without the job title), you are able to synthesize all the facts and facets, pounce on what's relevant and reveal all the subconscious or hidden information. *Voilà!*

Of course you're bored by superficial talk. That's not to say that you can't engage in it, just that you come out with the one-liner that renders all other banter meaningless! Those witty observations that are capable of striking to the core make other people well aware of your strong mental capacities and unflinching search for the real story. Once engaged, you'll leave no stone unturned in your search to know everything. This passion can make itself felt and cause other people to look more deeply too.

Soul Gift: Insight.
Unlocking Your Cosmic Potential: Enjoying the lighter topics in life makes a beautiful and valuable contrast to the deep and meaningful.

....

Mercury in Sagittarius ♐

You're a seeker. Possessing an open mind, you love to pick up knowledge from a variety of far-reaching sources and places that add to your lexicon of understanding. Funny, engaging and ultimately inspiring, you're a natural teacher and never stop learning either. Always looking for how an idea might develop, you encourage others to think big. You spot potential others might miss and are talented at taking things further, spreading the word and marketing the message. You're able to access cosmic wisdom, higher truth and knowledge seemingly out of nowhere.

Your enthusiasm and warmth encourage others to look on the bright side. You tend to have a philosophical approach to life that places everything in the big-picture context. For you, mental stimulation comes from other cultures and engaging with ideas that span the globe. Travel can be a big feature in your life and you are drawn to people who expand your horizons. The Law of Attraction is something you understand perfectly and can work to your advantage.

Soul Gift: Positive mental attitude.
Unlocking Your Cosmic Potential: Take time to examine the details and see how the macro is always reflected in the micro.

Mercury in Capricorn ♑

This is the planetary equivalent of the business mind. With Mercury in Capricorn, you have a canny sense of how to order, manage and manifest that results in a slow build towards success. Determined to apply yourself, you rarely shirk the effort involved in doing a good job. Your learning is thorough and well researched. Your delivery is professional and accomplished. You might not have the most enthralling of creative edges, but you're both practical and substantive.

You prefer order and routine to instant requests. Honing your mental skills enables you to rise to the top and you mistrust those who spin lines and promise a lot, as you suspect they will fail to deliver. Naturally cautious and circumspect, you pride yourself on living in the real world. You aren't given to flights of fancy and tend to stick to the tried and tested rather than branch out into the adventurous. You can easily find your niche within a hierarchy, taking steady steps up the ladder. You aren't the most effusive speaker, but your words carry weight and earn respect.

Soul Gift: Gravitas.
Unlocking Your Cosmic Potential: Defensive mental attitudes shut everything down. Instead, make the choice to open up.

Mercury in Aquarius ♒

You're the person who thinks outside the box. Easily coming up with original ideas, you're good at throwing a spanner into the works and breaking up old patterns. You have an affinity for new technology and can be at the forefront of developments, helping others to upgrade to the new paradigm. When it comes to an educational setting, you might find it hard to conform. Preferring to do things your way and bored by repetition, you can be ahead of the game, or simply wired differently from other minds, yet comfortable with logic and objectivity.

Fitting in with prevailing opinions is not your forte – you prefer to wake people up to something different, to introduce something that hasn't been done before or to explore avenues that people don't usually consider. You love to question everything and are both contrary and opinionated! You tend to speak without a filter. You refuse to be mentally stifled by consensus or tradition and have a genius for getting people excited, even if they aren't ready to take on your ideas. You have your finger on the pulse of what's going on in the collective.

Soul Gift: Ingenuity.
Unlocking Your Cosmic Potential: Abstract concepts and inventive ideas need practical application in order to become real.

Mercury in Pisces ♓

When the planet of the mind is resident in the sign most associated with fantasy, visual images and multidimensional thinking, you're able to access the creative and otherworldly realms more easily than most other people. You are actually quite capable of channelling your ideas from the ether, and do this unconsciously most of the time. For the same reason, you're able to pick up on how others are feeling and what's circulating in the atmosphere. You receive spiritual messages too. This can be wonderfully informative or confusing, depending on the messages you're receiving. You're connected to subtle nuance rather than logic. You see a million shades of grey where others see only black and white.

It can feel overwhelming to be so mentally open, and learning how to close down, have some boundaries and protect yourself enhances your capacity to think for yourself. Such a strong imagination and natural empathy and sensitivity incline you towards being able to heal with words and create magic with ideas. You might love dancing or be able to interpret what others want or think. This placement enables you to read people, yet you often find yourself disconnected from them, lost in thought or a dream world.

Soul Gift: Receptivity.

Unlocking Your Cosmic Potential: The mundane aspects of life can be imbued with creativity and magic if perceived with the eyes of the soul.

CHAPTER 7

Venus

Love, attraction, beauty, value

What does love mean to me?
What is my attraction factor
and soul connection style?

The mere mention of the word 'Venus' conjures up images of hearts and flowers, perhaps Cupid's arrows or Botticelli's 'Birth of Venus'. Love has so many forms and meanings, and our Venus sign (♀ in your chart) will reveal exactly how it takes shape for us.

Venus can open our heart or spark Cupid's chemistry, ignite unconditional love or fire up basic lust – anything from the rarified bliss of pure love to the shadow realm of toxic relationship. In ancient times, the goddess Venus was freed of any judgement, as she was perceived as an icon of feminine value, both divine and cutely come hither. It is only our projection of tangled personal complexes that conjures up the duality of sublime or erotic. The divine feminine is found in the art of relationships and is present in friendship, love and sex, as well as beauty and the arts. The divine feminine principle is based on magnetic energy that attracts and receives rather than propels and pursues. Venus emits a huge force of attraction.

Venus is a pivotal planet because it says so much about the personal choices we make, which are so often based on what we value. We spend our money on what we consider to be of value, whilst our self-esteem is based on how much we believe ourselves to be of value. So, Venus is involved with our price-point on the material side and our soul connection on a more esoteric level.

Our Venus sign reveals whether we feel we are, or someone else is, 'worth it'.

Venus is the conduit for what makes us happy and also how we believe we can make other people feel happy. Understanding our Venus enables us to steer our love destiny to its highest level.

We express our love and affection through our Venus sign, yet the other person's Venus may not be tuned to the same frequency. In other words, if we have Venus in an Earth sign (Taurus, Virgo or Capricorn), we believe physical affection and the simple things we do for each other are the foremost expression of love, whilst Venus in a Water sign (Cancer, Scorpio or Pisces) is longing for emotional intimacy and an exchange of feeling. Venus in a Fire sign (Aries, Leo or Sagittarius) thrives on high-voltage exchange and action, whilst Venus in Air (Gemini, Libra or Aquarius) is all about mental sparks and communication. It's really helpful to speak the love language of the other person's Venus element if we want our *amour* to feel loved!

No matter which gender or sexual orientation we are, Venus will tell us about our relationship with the feminine and what we find beautiful. It will show up on the outside in our personal style, the way we dress, how we 'present' ourselves. It will show up on the inside as our love code and blueprint.

***Venus holds all our secret desires
and what feels good to us.***

We need to access this inner Venus and allow this divine feminine energy to help us connect in relationships. Our love patterns are in our Venus sign!

Venus is our initial attraction factor, but its energetic vibration is also omnipresent once we get into a relationship. It shows our capacity for intimacy, romance, what we value in someone, how we might share, what kind of emotional energy feels loving to us and what we give out as an expression of love. Venus shows us what makes us feel affirmed by others.

Venus in the Shadow

So, if Venus is grace and flow, perfect symmetry, art, love and harmony, what about toxic relationships? What happens when we get involved with emotional vampires, narcissists, sociopaths? When we feel betrayed or abandoned, or love a person who is unavailable or unable to love us in the way we want?

If all's fair in love and war, then Venus will magnetize what's on our frequency, whether we say we want it or not. We can say we want a gentle, considerate partner, but perhaps we've got a secret Venus blueprint for drama that stirs up conflict, and hey presto, the difficult person keeps showing up, despite our protestations that we don't want this type of issue in our life. Unconsciously, we are sending out vibes that attract the lower vibration of our Venus. This is because we don't know how to integrate its shadow side. We are stuck in the groove of our love pattern, which is often rooted in childhood experiences.

We need to realize that it isn't life itself that needs to change, it's us!

We can up-level our Venus experience of love from vampire to validation simply by realizing we have the power to choose from our highest, most wide-awake place, rather than accepting the autopilot, low-frequency, snooze pattern.

Soul Connection Codes

Think for a moment about the possibility of being born in this life having already pre-ordered certain assignments with significant others. Relationships of all kinds make more sense when seen as soul contracts – mutual agreements that someone will play a particular role, initiate a certain experience, help us learn something we couldn't have experienced without their intervention. This is karma. For every action, there is a reaction, which extends beyond one lifetime but encompasses the many lifetimes of the soul. Someone could be in our life to trigger an experience that's for our highest good, no matter how painful it feels to the ego. It's possible that our soul-mate is the person that's capable of bringing up the greatest suffering. Even a fleeting relationship can trigger enormous awakening. Dropping the mindset that relationships are there to give us what we 'want', satisfy our ego and tick our boxes means we don't feed ourselves with expectations and control patterns that lead to disappointment.

If we can see another person through the eyes of the soul, then every experience we have is deeply meaningful and offers the opportunity to learn more about the true nature of love. Every person we are in a relationship with is there for our personal and soul development. They are there so we can grow. This awareness is so empowering and enables us to realize our potential for love. Withdrawing our projections of blame and victimization, we recognize what's really going on.

> *Every single relationship is an assignment. Its purpose is to teach us what we need to learn.*

Once we've learned the lesson, we can move forward. In this respect, every single connection is meaningful.

In encouraging us onto a path of self-awareness, discernment, self-esteem and higher love, Venus offers a magical mix that helps us make better choices. True intimacy requires a certain level of vulnerability, but if we approach it with self-esteem, then we're not afraid to go there. Instead of playing games or defending, rushing or inflicting wounds, we can see love as the biggest facilitator of our experience of the divine feminine.

> *Becoming who we are meant to be is to move into the highest vibration of love.*

Venus Retrograde

Approximately every two years, Venus goes retrograde, offering us all an opportunity to cleanse our perception of love. During the retrograde phase it's common to rethink, re-evaluate and/or reaffirm our closest relationships. Our relationship patterns become more obvious to us, as this time sheds light on what we're missing, seeking and valuing. If we're willing to become aware of what we've been doing, how we've been relating and what theme keeps repeating, we can review our patterns and grow. Venus retrogrades can often facilitate a great healing of the heart.

Venus Love Destiny

 Our Venus sign corresponds to what and whom we value, like, love and find attractive, beautiful and pleasurable.

So, take a look at your Venus sign. First of all, it illuminates you and your relationship with yourself and the feminine. It gives you insight into your personal love and relationship blueprint.

Venus in Aries ♀ ♈

Impulsive and spontaneous, you tend to rush into relationships, not being able to help yourself because you feel such an instant rush of attraction. It's eyes across a crowded room, that spark of chemistry that ignites the love bug. You almost pride yourself on how quickly things can take off. You are very direct in your love language, so you'll let someone know immediately that you find them attractive. Not for you the slow seduction, the games of courtship. You are a hunter – and the object of your desire hardly stands a chance if you're in pursuit. Sweeping someone off their feet comes naturally to you. In fact you are puzzled by other people's tales of indecision or their waiting games.

You like to get on with it, so your dating style tends to be active. You want to 'do things' with your partner, as you adore that sense of attraction when you see them in action. As you like to conquer, those who play hard to get can stimulate your interest. You're never attracted to losers – you like strong people who aren't afraid to compete in the cut and thrust of the world.

If you like someone, they'll know about it, as you're honest and upfront, but you'll lose interest if things don't go somewhere. You want to win someone, to be admired. If the object of your desire isn't essentially 'up for it', you tend to fall away. Your love blueprint likes challenge and high energy, so a poetic nature might be lost on you.

Love Style: Vibrant, ardent, spontaneous, sparky, instigating.
Cosmic Potential: Can I appreciate both the sparks and the eternal flame?

Venus in Taurus ♉

Sensual and slow, you take time in forming relationships, preferring things to be built up gradually rather than rushed. You exude a deliciously physical magnetic attraction – your body has a perfection and sensuality. Touch is a vitally important sense for you and the number-one means of conveying your feelings. A hug with you speaks volumes and puts the entire world to rights.

As an Earth sign, Taurus is looking for security, and therefore you want to know where you stand and if the other person is capable of attaching properly, by which you mean long-term commitment. Earth is practical, therefore you do enough due diligence to find out if the relationship will work on a material and emotional level.

Once involved, it takes a lot to put you off. You have a stubborn side to your nature that doesn't give up. This is why you'll make every effort to ensure the relationship works, long after others would have pulled the plug. You'll hang in there, believing that enduring difficulties is a small price to pay for a long-lasting partnership.

Loyal and dedicated, you are also prepared to put on blinkers to tune out the less desirable aspects of a relationship. As long as there is food on the table and another pair of toes in the bed, that's fine. You appreciate routine and rhythm, and find it hard to understand why anyone would want to experiment. You aren't looking for constant excitement, but durability, the pleasures of the senses and simple enjoyments.

Love Style: Sensual, affectionate, dependable, supportive.
Cosmic Potential: Can I open my heart to love expressed in myriad ways, not just by commitment?

Venus in Gemini ♊

The most flirtatious Venus! You're the chat-up maestro, dizzyingly dazzling with your wit and repartee and sheer capacity to jump from one subject to another. Come to think of it, from one person to another, as your interest can be caught and then lost very easily. You're light-hearted, and this comes across in your love frequency, which is bubbly and sparkling. When things fall flat, you find it hard to stick around.

As Gemini is the sign of duality, there can be two sides to you that others find both interesting and unnerving. You can spin, change direction, change sides – which can be interpreted as disloyalty – and are always on the move and can't be pinned down to just one form, idea, action, or even person. If you are accused of shallowness, it's because you literally don't have time to explore things very deeply and you have no desire to get trapped in heavy situations.

Basically, you're the person who gets the party started. The fun begins when you enter the room and your playfulness is much sought after, which is why you're the consummate people person. This makes a one-to-one relationship hard for you, as you need so much variety, room to breathe and social contact. Keeping things interesting is the bottom line in any form of relationship for you. Having such a low boredom threshold makes it vital that you're with someone who matches your curiosity and engagement with life and can give you the space to socialize and explore what's out there. A meeting of minds is essential.

Love Style: Bright, breezy, talkative, engaging.
Cosmic Potential: Can I keep the conversation going with my beloved?

Venus in Cancer ♋

Venus in the sign of the emotionally intelligent crab provides a huge reservoir of nurturing empathy. You really 'get' people. You read them. You know what they need. Your great gift is being able to pick up on what pleases them, and you can transfer love in a variety of forms, as your Water element shapeshifts to meet what's required. You have a lot of love to give. You like to take care of people, look after them and bring out the best in them. Yet there's an aspect of this kind of devotional energy that feels too much for some of the Venus in Fire or Air sign types. If you're constantly 'on tap' for them, their instinct is to turn you off! This isn't necessarily a rejection, just a need for space, for room to breathe.

Your reassuring presence is, however, extremely comforting and protective. You are a gentle soul in love, longing for the emotional embrace, the intuitive understanding and the intimacy. You cling to people you care about, which others may interpret as being needy, yet your pincers can't let go very easily. When hurt, you tend to retreat inside your shell and can be moodily defensive. Yet if you feel safe in a relationship, you can create the emotional glue that connects two souls forever. The emotional comfort zone you provide is second to none, your intuition spot on. You fall in love instinctively rather than through the mind, as your radar can read the matching of frequencies. Home, family and personal life will always come first for you, hence one of your biggest criteria for the love signal is whether or not you feel at home with someone.

Love Style: Caring, nurturing, aware, tender, sustaining.
Cosmic Potential: Can I empathize and care whilst letting go?

Venus in Leo ♌

Big-hearted Venus in Leo is a love vibration that ignites strong passions and warmth that lights up the room. This Venus is a true spark of love that catches fire. As the royal sign, you command unwavering attention from your suitors and a certain amount of special treatment. You want to be adored, even worshipped! You can be quite high-maintenance in this respect, yet you have such a generous spirit and an exuberant love of life that people light up when you're around.

You appreciate the best of everything, so it's fortunate you possess a certain style that magnetizes life's luxuries and abundance. It could be that nothing is ever enough for you and others find you demanding – but then you create unforgettable, show-stopping magnificence and a tremendous sense of occasion that lifts spirits and warms hearts.

In love, you must be number one – nothing less will do. For you, love is a consuming passion, a grand vision and a romantic affair, and if it ever loses its lustre, you visibly wilt. You don't do well with those who burst your romantic bubble. The mundane aspects of being in a relationship don't sit so well with you either – your fire is put out by any perceived loss of interest or any kind of boring, thankless, repetitive task. Yet you're so responsive to attention – quite literally the big cat that purrs with delight – that your happiness is infectious, and your giving is of a show-stopper quality! You like to live and love in style. What's vital for you is keeping the dream alive in a relationship – and on a grand scale.

Love Style: Radiant, effusive, showy, heartfelt.
Cosmic Potential: Can I appreciate another person without making myself the centre of attention?

Venus in Virgo ♍

Here we have the true vestal virgin, who makes themselves available as an act of giving and service. With Venus here, you are a kind, hard-working, thoughtful lover who may not be big on special effects but knows how to keep the wheels turning.

You're picky! Because you cannot help but observe every little detail about another person. You see their flaws and faults, and you see your own, and that is why you're so busily engaged in trying to weave together a better state of perfection.

Your quality control hinges on the mind. You enjoy a meeting of minds. For you, attraction begins in the mind, and as long as this level of engagement continues to hold your interest, you'll be there. Of course, as Virgo is the sign of anxiety, you can't help fretting and worrying over what might happen, which engenders a less than relaxed atmosphere between you and your loved one. Getting out of your mind and into your heart is essential, but not your default setting.

Your natural sense of refinement is repelled by the gross and crude. You're gentle in nature, yet, as an Earth sign, possessed of great natural resources and strength. A sense of orderliness permeates your approach to life and love, a feeling of 'everything in its place'. Yet the ways of the heart can be chaotic, unreasonable and unfathomable, and your attempts to control them through answering people's practical needs may somehow miss the point of your connection. Analysis may give you clues as to where to go in a relationship, yet being able to trust your heart is the real journey.

Love Style: Considerate, understated, astute, with high standards.
Cosmic Potential: Can I relax into my heart without my thoughts getting in the way?

....

Venus in Libra ♎

The charm of Venus in Libra is legendary. You can get people to eat out of the palm of your hand, as Venus is in its natural domain here. Yet any relationship has to conform to your rules of engagement. No nasties; nothing uncouth, ugly or too wayward. For you, love is all about aesthetics and politesse. Put simply, it's very important to you to be liked and you are a consummate people-pleaser.

Your social skills work well in groups and negotiation. You smooth out difficulties and neutralize discord. One to one, you experience the true balancing of your scales and you tend to attract your opposite in order to experience the micro-shifts that create the adjustments you enjoy performing in relationships. Fairness is a big deal for you, so anyone who tips your scales too much leaves you struggling for balance. Yet you enjoy a challenge, even a sparring match, as an Air sign Venus is stimulated by verbal exchange and the frisson of differing points of view.

Beauty and gracefulness fuel your idealistic Venus, which feels at its best in romantic settings and is the natural stylist of the zodiac. Love can be your drug, yet you would do anything to avoid unpleasant feelings. For you, compatibility means entering into the dance of relating. Seeing yourself in relation to another is actually helpful to you in terms of understanding who you are. It is a rare Venus in Libra who enjoys being alone. You much prefer relating! You actually find it hard to say 'no' and your gift for adjusting to others means that you can fit in with them to the point of losing what's important for you.

Love Style: Romantic, sociable, diplomatic, compromising.
Cosmic Potential: Can I truly be myself in relation to another?

Venus in Scorpio ♏

True connection for you goes very deep – you long for total union on an emotional and spiritual level. Although you can shut down from those who threaten to expose, hurt or contaminate you, your healing power stems from being able to bare your soul to another. For you, the meaning of sharing is both intangible and tangible, involving layers of trust and the capacity to transform yourself and others.

Your mysterious allure stems from your highly charged yet hidden energy. It can be sensed as a frequency that separates you from the rest of the crowd. For you, awareness is everything – you find it deeply attractive. Complicated situations don't bother you, it's the shallow and superficial that repel. Those who prefer surface relationships find you intriguing and rather challenging. Your love frequency always wants to go deeper, to discover and explore the innermost desires, drives, nuances, hurts and soul path. You can be all or nothing too – the middle ground doesn't appeal. You possess a sixth sense that instantly recognizes a soul contract between one person and another.

Your vibration is essentially magnetic and meaningful and you can convey a profound insight in a one-liner that leaves people wondering how on Earth you knew that. You get a bad rap for your 'sting' when in fact you are more often stung to the quick by less sensitive souls. You are an alchemist, mixing together the love ingredients in two people in search of a profound union, true gold. Your inner strength and knowing can save you from any burns or poisoning in the process.

Love Style: Intense, deeply soulful, transformative.
Cosmic Potential: Can I trust my heart and grow through relationship?

....

Venus in Sagittarius ♐

Playful and fun-loving, Venus in the sign of the archer loves the chase. Firing off arrows as the mood takes you, then riding off after the next target, you can be quite the party animal, a pleasure-seeking hedonist, yet your soul calls out for something more meaningful. Ultimately, you create a philosophy from the search for and experience of love.

Your love journey towards wisdom encompasses wide horizons, as Sagittarius is the traveller, so you're naturally attracted to people and places that have something to offer in terms of cultural exchange. Besides which, your optimistic and opportunistic nature believes something wonderful is always around the corner and you have a way of maximizing your potential whenever possible. You may seem to be born under a lucky star, but that doesn't mean you're immune to heartbreak or disappointment, just that you generally maintain a positive outlook and don't tend to wallow in the past. It's a gift that serves you well in terms of the Law of Attraction. Seemingly, Venus smiles on you. Perhaps, though, you're simply more appreciative of what life and love have to offer.

For you, love must be a life-enhancing adventure. You tend to go in enthusiastically, as per your Fire sign energy, creating smiles and good times. Exuberant and energetic, you like to do things with people, so a sedentary partner isn't ideal for you. Keeping you amused is no easy feat, so commitment must come with its lighter moments. The great outdoors appeals to you and you're the kind of person to take off spontaneously rather than formulate plans. You may have well-meaning but tactless moments, but your sheer warmth and generosity offset them – and anyway, it was all a joke, wasn't it?!

Love Style: Adventurous, positive, warm, playful.

Cosmic Potential: Can I open up to love's continuity and enjoy exploring it without always changing the scenery?

Venus in Capricorn ♑

Love is a serious business for you. You're not one to flit between relationships or surprise everyone with an 'odd couple' pairing. Or even let anyone through your very strong boundaries. Venus here can be surprisingly shy about getting close. It only happens after careful consideration and assessment. You possess a business sense that says relationships should be mutually beneficial and serve a purpose. Therefore you conduct a risk analysis before entering into a relationship, including the gains and losses in status, finances and reward for effort. Building a solid partnership that lasts is your goal.

Self-control is your default setting, so you need the other person to relax your resistance! However, your coolness can be magnetic to those who seek out your contained, responsible frequency. More uptight when younger, you may ripen late, but you're good at looking after others and commitment is your goal – which has its upside! Making the effort, doing the hard work and solving problems is second nature to you – an asset that has long-term value over pure romance. Not one to idealize others, you see the reality of a relationship, though, and your Venus reflexes shut down if you sense danger or lack of respect.

Venus in Capricorn is a frequency for the love connoisseur, the grown-up, not the immature attention-seeker. Whilst some people may find you rather chilly or hard, you can't help being matter-of-fact, even in love. Unless your heart opens, you will find yourself left out in the cold. Better to exchange your permafrost for permanence in the relationship department and begin your climb up the mountain of love.

Love Style: Proper, reliable, real, supportive.
Cosmic Potential: Can I open my heart whilst retaining my pragmatism?

Venus in Aquarius ≈

Venus here, in the coolest of Air signs, tends to value friendship and the meeting of minds over the more sentimental aspects of love. You have a quirky, out-of-the-box mindset that extends to affairs of the heart, thereby attracting you to the unusual. You don't like to conform to preconceived ideas of what love should look like. Yours is a more universal frequency, unbounded by the protocols of rhyme and reason. Free spirits, some of you simply don't want to get tied down. Others are not entirely no-strings, but soul strings – that connect you to a love that may not fit convention but makes your heart sing and keeps the excitement, which is your number-one priority.

You're not given to expressing yourself with hearts and flowers – the stirrings of love will be conveyed in your own unique way! Aquarius has an electrical frequency that works almost telepathically, but its current is erratic and tends to switch on and off. So, in your contrary, contradictory way, you are the most tolerant and intolerant, connected and disconnected Venus sign on the planet!

Being in a routine feels imprisoning, so you like to have breathing space in your relationship and a lot of other people on the periphery. As friendship is so important to you, let this be the bedrock of a relationship.

Your unusual take on love is very refreshing and you often act as an awakener for more conventional people. Your timing is entirely your own, you cut through whatever is expected and do it your way. You are both impersonal yet highly sensitive, super-friendly yet detached. It's possible for you to channel flashes of intuition directly from the fifth dimension that take love to a universal level of truth.

Love Style: Open, exciting, detached, independent.
Cosmic Potential: Can I move from friendship to intimacy?

....

Venus in Pisces ♓

The unbounded, oceanic nature of Venus in Pisces flows into all areas, finding ways around rocks and boulders, and seeping through seemingly solid boundaries. Channelling unconditional love is your highest attribute, yet your psyche can pick up contamination and become polluted, toxic and stagnant if you haven't installed a filter or natural purification system! Basically, you need boundaries, discernment and discrimination. Otherwise, you can pour out your love sacrificially, co-dependently or addictively, thereby reducing its highest vibration to a damaging frequency.

Having said that, you are the most romantic and idealistic of all Venus signs, searching for enchantment, rapture, bliss and escapism. You have abundant emotional intelligence and empathy and absorb other people's feelings. In some ways you seek a romantic bubble that elevates you from the ordinary, yet until you accept reality there is always the possibility of disappointment. Perhaps sensing that humans find it hard to be capable of unconditional love 24/7, you can also have an avoidant style of relating where you yearn for love, yet pick unavailable people. Or perhaps swim in two directions, leaving a partner confused as to where you are.

You have a love blueprint that can experience absolute fusion with another person, reaching a level of transcendence few will ever attain. You can heal with your accepting, gentle approach. Yet you have to steer clear of getting lost in other people, giving so much that they become overwhelmed and abandoning. The most important thing you can do is to anchor and ground yourself so that the love drug doesn't create a need that is impossible to fulfil. Intuitively, you can read what's going on, so take those messages as clear instructions!

Love Style: Seductive, surrendering, magical, mystical.
Cosmic Potential: Can I create a safe space for my heart?

CHAPTER 8

Mars

Driving force, energy, sense of purpose,
will, way of making things happen

How do I manifest my soul purpose?
What do I need to achieve?
How are my desires expressed in the world?

Mars (♂ in your chart) is the macho god of war, battle, desire, striving and fierce competition. He is fairly primitive in that he wants what he wants and he wants it *now*. Regardless of niceties or casualties. Giving Mars full rein would be akin to letting our most grabbing instincts have their way. Yet we need Mars energy, as we can't access our willpower without it. It gives us the gift of manifestation, yet we need to ask what it is we really want from a deeper place than the small self. From a place of soul purpose.

Primarily a male, yang energy, Mars can act like a Neanderthal or express the divine masculine. This planet is inflammatory, even conflict-prone, but the source of our vitality. The strength and authority of Mars are much needed; this active energy moves our lives forward, giving us courage and the initiative to take the next step.

If we don't get in touch with our Mars and remain passive, then it's easy to blame others for everything and to become helpless or depressed. Mars is our fighting spirit, our get-up-and-go. The planet's placement in our chart describes how we can take control of our destiny by living the purpose of who we came here to be.

Having a good relationship with our Mars connects us to our power of choice. We can get on with our lives, stand up for ourselves when we need to and we have a healthy enough ego to know what we want. Not knowing what we want is a repression of Mars, which cuts off our capacity to act and drains our vital life-force.

A repressed, depressed Mars
can suck the life out of us and lead
to many mental health issues.

It's interesting that beneath depression lies anger, which is what we feel when we aren't able to express Mars energy. Frustration, numbness, detachment and inner deadness, lack of energy or desire are sure signs that our Mars is blocked and not functioning in a healthy way.

On the other hand, Mars energy on the rampage can create a great deal of negative karma. This alpha energy needs to be tamed, trained and channelled into something positive. Left to its own devices, it can turn sulky, resentful or bullying.

If Mars is unconscious in us, we do things without taking responsibility for our actions and we may be passive-aggressive because we can't own our desires. If we acknowledge and harness this energy, we can use it to achieve goals, move mountains and accomplish great things, both in the world and in our own life. Potency and agency stream through us and we rise to the challenges that are presented to us.

> *We can either let our ego desires run the show and act selfishly, or align with the soul and channel our Mars into manifesting our life purpose.*

The sign Mars is in can also say a lot about how we express our sexual desire – through a conquest (Mars in Aries) or a romantic dance (Mars in Libra).

The Mars Return

Mars returns to the place it was in when we were born at approximately 24 months. This period coincides with the so-called 'terrible twos', when the toddler strives to assert their will. Thereafter, Mars will return to its natal position approximately every two years, giving us a chance to reaffirm ourselves and receive new universal energy codes which unlock our cosmic potential.

Mars Retrograde

When Mars turns retrograde, which happens approximately every two years for a period of two and a half months, we play catch-up with unresolved issues. This can be a period of thwarted desires, as the wheels of life seemingly stop turning and it can feel impossible to get things done. However, it's an important period for calling time on all that is not meant to be. Especially if we've been hanging on, but the situation is clearly on life support.

This isn't always easy. Mars retrograde both challenges and strengthens our willpower and resolve. It also brings up our old battles, conflicts and grudges!

But Mars retrograde is an opportunity to let go,
make our peace and heal our ego wounds.

Counter-intuitively, the greatest act of personal choice is to surrender to the impossibility of situations that just drain our energy. A clear-out enables us to access fresh energy and start over, full of intention and purpose.

Mars Manifesting

Mars describes what we want and
how we make it happen.

So now let's look at the sign position of your Mars and discover what you want and how you make it happen.

Mars in Aries ♈

Dynamic Mars has its natural home in forthright Aries. It's a fiery, feisty combo that drives you on, no matter if you're a gentle Sun in Pisces or practical Moon in Taurus. Impatience is your default setting – anything that slows you down is to be pushed out of your way. A natural-born leader, entrepreneur, single-handed start-up person, you're never short of goals. Yet the mundane aspects of seeing them through are best delegated to those who enjoy repetitive tasks and management.

You fire others with your enthusiasm, so you're best as an initiator. It's your spirit of enterprise that gets projects off the ground. You're a can-do person, even a 'won't take no for an answer' type, which is helpful for sales and rallying the troops. When a need for collaboration arises, you do have to dial it down a bit, though, and listen to others.

For you, life is a game of winners and losers – and you want to win at all costs. Proving yourself to be better than others is irresistible. You come across as a strong person, wanting to do things your way and thriving on challenges. You're not averse to arguments either. For you, a straightforward set-to will clear the air, then quickly be forgotten as you move on to the next thing.

Soul Desire: To bravely thrust forward in life.
How You Make Things Happen: Assertive, independent, go-getting.

Mars in Taurus ♉

Solid and stable, you go about getting what you want in a firm and steady manner, with a great sense of purpose. You don't give up easily – once you're committed to doing something, you're there for the duration. Of course, you may possess surface layers of mercurial Sun in Gemini or exuberant Moon in Sagittarius, but when it comes to making something happen, you knuckle down to the task in hand.

Your fixity is unswerving, your loyalty unquestionable. Therefore people depend on you.

Whilst you keep on going, no matter what, of course you do meet frustrations and challenges. Yet you possess a robust perseverance that sees you through them, an inner strength that is rock-like. Your earthy qualities are all about sustaining and preserving, and therefore you won't fly off the handle at the slightest obstacle. Of course, it can be difficult to get you to change course once you've made up your mind to do something. You find it hard to let go, even if something clearly isn't working. And it takes a lot to rile you, but of course a red rag will eventually cause a bull to charge.

One of your attributes is the capacity to get on with things without needing either attention or instant results, as you enjoy the process of building something and tending to it. Blessed with common sense, you have a practical streak that grounds you even when others are in panic mode.

Soul Desire: Long-term stability and security.
How You Make Things Happen: Steady, reliable, grounded.

Mars in Gemini ♊

With Mars in Gemini, you see life as a playground of possibilities and chase after a million things at once. Many capture your curiosity, then bite the dust as you speed on to the next object of interest. Essentially a multitasker, you find it perfectly possible to do two or three jobs at once; in fact, switching between interests keeps you lively and fresh. You love people, therefore it's important for you to work with them, talk with them, mix and mingle with them as much as possible. You are particularly interested in transmitting news and information, so the media world can have a special appeal for you.

Knuckling down to a single task is not your favourite occupation, especially if it involves repetition or concentration without interruption. Your forte is to dazzle with a new take on how to do things, how to add interesting information to the mix. You want to feel connected with others and part of the plan, rather than quietly getting on with your own thing. Being a networker, you can light up a roomful of people or lift the engagement level at a meeting. Your sparkly energy livens up any proceedings! Your strength is in being able to talk to anyone about anything, and being naturally interested in people, you're never lost for questions or points of connection. You live in a world of words and information!

Soul Desire: To find out as much as possible.
How You Make Things Happen: Verbal, persuasive, eloquent.

Mars in Cancer ♋

In the watery realm of Cancer, Mars has to learn to read the currents and swim with them. Mars energy is all about individual wants, yet in the caretaking sign of Cancer can be transmuted into fulfilling what other people want or need. This is not to say that if you have Mars here you should sacrifice your own desires – in fact, the whole purpose of Mars in Cancer is to find what is resonant with the self and to take care of that as a primary need. Yet your sensitivity towards others often leads you to subvert what you want if others make a big deal of their own desires.

As said before, you have to learn to read the currents – in particular the unspoken emotional desires and issues that hang in the atmosphere. You're one step ahead if you get these and can produce what Buddhists would call the right action at the right time. This takes great skill, involving a perfect blending of what you can offer with what is needed without creating any karma!

You enjoy being a provider and protector. Having many people, whether family, cohorts or friends, under your wing, or your crab shell, gives you a sense of worth. In this respect you act a bit like a guard dog. You can get all huffy if you feel unappreciated – a lunar-ruled Mars can get crabby and defensive – but when you're in full flow from a place of self-esteem, no one can diminish your tender intentions.

Soul Desire: To establish soul bonds.
How You Make Things Happen: Intuitive, supportive, with emotional intelligence.

....

Mars in Leo ♌

Placed in the most show-offy of signs, Mars struts its stuff energetically and creatively. Being naturally drawn to the bright lights and the best, you don't do banal or ordinary. You can have an appetite for attention and ego-stroking, likes and admiration, but your soul lesson is to operate at your best capacity without being at the mercy of the response you get.

Leo loves colour and magnificence, and you don't do well in the back room or a low-key setting, as it deprives you of the limelight. You have a pride in your abilities that can be injured if you feel overlooked. Ideally, you need a platform that gives you creative *carte blanche*. Whatever you do, your intention is to be impressive. To create the wow-factor.

You can't help being competitive, but it's not the challenge of other people that drives you, but the desire to be recognized and adored. You can also be overbearing, as you can't help believing that you do know best and are more deserving than others. However, when you shine, there is no other Mars sign that is so radiant and spectacular.

Soul Desire: To attract attention and love.
How You Make Things Happen: Extravagant, charismatic, centre-stage.

....

Mars in Virgo ♍

The most finickity of signs, Virgo is the master curator and connoisseur. With Mars here, you have high standards and a critical eye that mean that it's hard for others to live up to your expectations, and you will never rest, never let up, even just for a minute. It's not that you're overtly demanding, as Virgo isn't a *prima donna*. But you notice every little fault and can't help pointing it out. This can make you a hard task-master, but very self-critical too.

Attention to detail is your stock-in-trade. Nothing escapes your notice, and your sense of responsibility is channelled into undertaking everything to the very best of your ability. Therefore, you're renowned for doing a good job – in fact, for a level of perfectionism that is rarely seen. Even so, you find yourself thinking, 'Could do better.' You're the worker bee, looking to see where you can help, organize and fix. Make things run smoothly for others. Efficient Virgo displays a devotion to the task and level of service to others that carries a sense of selflessness. With Mars in this sign, you're a true giver. Quite simply, you enjoy doing things for others.

Discernment is a special talent of yours, as is an eye for detail. Planning and preparation come naturally. You're into routines, rituals, good health habits and making yourself useful. This doesn't necessarily make you a saint, but it minimizes the dramas of the ego. Still, you can over-analyze and fret unless you learn how to relax your need for control.

Soul Desire: To attain perfection.
How You Make Things Happen: Careful, critical, astute, ordered.

Mars in Libra ♎

Doing things with grace and style is hugely important to you. If it can't be done beautifully and elegantly, then it is of little value to you. The way you conduct yourself, engage with the world and go about your business carries a sense of harmony and refinement. Not for you the crass pushiness, the arrogance, primitive qualities and bad manners that you consider the ultimate in ugly behaviour. Instead you tap into a wealth of charm and diplomacy, not to mention social skills, that smooth your path.

Avoiding battles is one of your objectives. You prefer to be liked, to get where you're going without ruffling feathers. It can be hard for you to assert yourself, to do what's best for you, as you're always considering what's fair or in everyone's interests. This can lead to an inability to make a move, or even a decision, and you may find others jumping in front of you to get what they want.

However, when it comes to any kind of negotiating, resolving differences or neutralizing them, your special powers are much admired. You have a talent for finding ways to promote cooperation and agreement. You're also very good at simply getting people to relate to each other, because you understand how to compare and contrast, to find common ground. There is an artistry at work here, a social grace that stems from the Libran appreciation of proportion, etiquette and balance.

Soul Desire: To foster goodwill and fairness.
How You Make Things Happen: Charming, accommodating, fair.

Mars in Scorpio ♏

Passion drives everything you do and you tend to see things in black and white, so you are either throwing yourself in wholeheartedly or considering it 'not your thing'. There is no Mars sign more resilient or with such hidden depths, yet your superpowers may be hidden or played close to your chest and largely unrecognized until people know you very well or see the results of your efforts. This suits you, as you prefer to operate under your own steam without the need for a big shout-out. You have a real gift for turning things around and creating something wonderful from what's been discarded or damaged. You understand the art of transformation and use it to good effect, breathing new life into people and projects. You can rise like a phoenix from the ashes, and so can anyone or anything that comes under your wing.

Single-minded and determined, you possess an inner self-control that filters out non-essentials on the pathway to achieving your desires. Your all-or-nothing approach can be both steely and soft, yet it's your intuition that guides you along the right lines. Digging deep is your preferred route, so you undertake forensic analysis and research. Performing complicated tasks with ease and with an incredible talent for synthesizing complex information to produce the salient points, you see – with X-ray vision – straight through to the absolute truth.

Proving yourself and controlling the outcome are your driving forces and you can become obsessive in pursuit of your goals. Drawn to the deep and meaningful rather than the shallow and superficial, you will find your challenge is to handle your powerful desires and resources whilst taking the higher path.

Soul Desire: To magnetize all that is meant for you.
How You Make Things Happen: Determined, intuitive, alchemical – turning base matter into gold.

Mars in Sagittarius ♐

An adventurous spirit lies inside you. You can't wait to explore all the world has to offer and to seize all the opportunities available. You may fire off arrows of desire in all directions and never stop moving long enough to ground and stabilize yourself, yet you're a source of inspiration for those who give up hope too easily. Playful by nature, you'd be bored in a rigidly contained and structured setting, and itchy feet would get the better of you, so it's best to ensure you always have space and room to manoeuvre.

You cover a lot of ground both mentally and physically, refusing to accept barriers and limitations. In this sense you are something of an explorer, always searching on the far-distant horizon for the next best thing. Going global appeals to you, as being stuck in one place feels like a prison.

Being future-oriented enables you to see where and how things could develop, which is useful for spotting what's opening up and making the most of business opportunities. You're a risk-taker, an optimist, and this can at times translate into carelessness and lack of forethought. But when you get to be the wise centaur, you use your wisdom and engage in the right thing at the right time.

Being spontaneous and playful, enthusiastic and generous-spirited aligns you with the Law of Attraction, so that it appears you have all the luck. However, you can blow it if you constantly chance your arm without reining yourself in to check things out properly.

Soul Desire: To develop your potential.
How You Make Things Happen: Optimistic, positive, brave, adventurous.

Mars in Capricorn ♑

Few people possess your very grown-up sense of purpose and self-discipline. Whilst others experiment and go off the rails, you keep tight control and direct your energy into reaching your mountain peak. You're the person with a plan, a goal, a strategy that is both practical and wise. What's more, you're determined to put in the effort. You will get there, no matter what it takes. Uphill struggles don't bother you; in fact, you recognize them for what they are – workouts for your willpower and valuable tests of your expertise. Not expecting things to land in your lap, you don't look for any kind of special treatment. Even lucky breaks are treated with circumspection, as you prefer to work for something and know you truly deserve it.

A strong desire for financial security and a position in life fuels your climb to the top. Along the way, you work long and hard and take on big responsibilities, your management skills coming to the fore as you dedicate yourself to organizing and orchestrating other people.

You tend to put the job first and your personal life second, which means it's hard for you to switch off. Practical and sensible by nature, you want to do things properly. With your good business head as your guide, in the end you come out with something to show for your efforts, without having risked all for nothing.

Soul Desire: To achieve your goal.
How You Make Things Happen: Practical, responsible, ambitious, controlled.

Mars in Aquarius ♒

You are a non-conformist. Whatever it is, you will do it differently. This can be a unique gift or a disruptive influence, yet you see disruption as a path to freedom. Others may not think so and attempt to clamp down on your predilection for breaking the rules. So, unless you see yourself as a radical activist, it is probably best to operate in a setting where it's possible to do your own thing, rather than have to fit into a fixed and long-established structure.

You're full of surprises and your unconventional approach can inspire others to think in radically new ways. You shake things up so tired old routines feel revitalized and fresh. Your way of revolutionizing things comes naturally to you but can come as a revelation to those who have got stuck in a rut. You like to deal with new material or a constant round of change that feeds your need for stimulation, and you're great with people and groups, but equally can go it alone. Friendly and curious, you're nonetheless able to detach when things spill into emotional territory and drama. There is a coolness to your approach – you're capable of cutting off and walking away. You view this as fulfilling your need for freedom and independence. Some people may view *you* as contrary or even impersonal. Certainly unpredictable.

Soul Desire: To do things your way.
How You Make Things Happen: Original, unusual, innovative.

Mars in Pisces ♂ ♓

When the action planet Mars is placed in the numinous sign of Pisces, the will is moving into transcendent territory. In other words, your ego is not your ultimate residence but simply a vehicle for your desires to reach a more superconscious plane through creativity, intuition, spirituality, healing, compassion and service. You don't follow a linear trajectory here, much less a well-defined plan. Instead, you *feel* what's right for you and the direction you should go in. Your intuition guides you.

In many ways, you find it hard to articulate and discern what you want, as Pisces is such a magical, mystical sign that what you want is subtle rather than obvious. You are drawn to the intangibles in life such as the creation of special effects, images, dance, music and healing. You have a giving nature, a connection with those who suffer and need your help.

Operating at a lower level, Mars in Pisces is so subtle that you can lose sight of the real world and things slip through your fingers. This is the most addictive and escapist of signs, so it's important to learn how to anchor yourself, establish good boundaries and be discriminating in your choices.

You go with the flow rather than fighting for what you want and even though you get lost at times, the art of surrender teaches you more than any land-grabs or Pyrrhic victories would. Slipping into the creative realm with immense ease, you can glimpse paradise there and bring it down to Earth.

Soul Desire: To follow your dreams.
How You Make Things Happen: Graceful, gentle, intuitive.

Part III

The Social Planets

The social planets, Jupiter and Saturn, represent the wider world and show how we interact with it. They also enable us to map the interplay between our karma and cosmic potential which is always a work of co-creation. They will, like the personal planets, be positioned in one of the 12 houses, according to our time of birth. Check the house diagram (*on page 22*) to find out in which area of life your social planets are positioned. It is within this setting that their energies will be active.

Next, look at your birth chart to see what matches your personal planets (Sun, Moon, Mercury, Venus and Mars) make with your social planets. See if there's a conjunction, sextile, trine, square or opposition between them.

- Conjunction ☌ – the planets are close together and have a strong combined impact
- Sextile ✳ – the planets are around 60 degrees apart, complement each other and promote mutual growth and harmony
- Trine △ – the planets are around 120 degrees apart and their energies flow together easily and effortlessly

- Square □ – the planets are around 90 degrees apart and tension arises between them, challenging us to reconcile different parts of ourselves

- Opposition ☍ – the planets are around 180 degrees apart and there is conflict between their energies

These aspects indicate you have a strong frequency match with that social planet. It's part of your soul plan! If you have no personal aspects to a particular social planet, its vibration will make its presence felt mainly through its sign and house position.

With the harmonious sextile or trine aspects, you are likely to be able to integrate the energies of the planet into your life readily and easily. You can flow with their meaning and purpose.

With the more challenging conjunction, square or opposition, there is work to be done, which may involve radical changes on your part. These soul codes indicate the need to wake up to these energies and transform yourself through experiencing their less conscious expression and up-levelling to their highest vibration.

With any major aspect between your personal and social planets, you have the specific soul intention to embody and live these energies as consciously as possible and use them to raise your frequency, wisdom and awareness.

 These aspects show how you can choose to up-level your destiny!

CHAPTER 9

Jupiter

Potential, opportunity, abundance, expansion

How do I expand my world?
How can I attract abundance and joy?

The largest planet in our solar system connects us to the realm of expansion, optimism, opportunity and joy. It encourages us to reach out and keep developing. When we tap into Jupiter (♃ in your chart), we align with the promise of an opportunity that will improve our quality of life. It's an opening. We're being given a chance, a stroke of luck, which inspires a positive upturn and an outpouring of faith in the goodness of life.

 Jupiter provides a vision of what might be and who we are here to become if we unlock our cosmic potential.

Of course, not every offer manifests as reality – we still have to land it. It's interesting that some people receive many lucky breaks and potential offers, but prefer to stay small. Others take opportunities for granted, or don't even see them. Yet it's possible to recognize a lucky break, seize it and up-level it into a major growth spurt. Relying solely on Jupiter to come up trumps may not work, but at the very least it inspires us to make the best of things. It encourages us to count our blessings in every way possible.

Jupiter attracts good times and puts us in good spirits.

Yet, as with all soul-level astrology, we have to look beyond what's happening in the material third dimension in order to pick up the full spectrum of frequencies available.

The sign Jupiter is in when we were born has a lot to offer us in the way of 'good karma'. We might have already built up some credits here on our soul's journey. Or perhaps through developing the qualities of Jupiter's sign we feel we're 'one of the lucky ones'. In terms of making our own luck, Jupiter's sign shows what comes to us naturally.

Jupiter even reflects our protection from above, our capacity to connect to the right spirit guides. With Jupiter's nudges towards our greater good, we're able to see who and what is being placed on our path as the 'helpers' on our unfolding hero's journey.

The Priest and the Playboy

In keeping with Zeus's open-all-areas policy, Jupiter is perhaps the ultimate mediator between heaven and Earth. Jupiter's many adventures can be experienced in terms of the high-living party animal on one level. Yet, an expansion in consciousness, similar to kundalini rising, brings Jupiter's quest to a more spiritual level of wisdom. His journey encompasses the heady combo of both the faith and the faithless in that respect! Astrologically, Jupiter can be exaggerated and hedonistic yet also wisely life-affirming. Once you recognize this pure expansive energy, you can choose where best to place it in your life.

The Law of Attraction – Manifesting Abundance and Creating Luck

Jupiter's power can be actively engaged in magnetizing what we wish to attract. In keeping with this positive frequency, one way to do this is to act 'as if' we are already experiencing what we desire. This neutralizes any fears or doubts about being undeserving. Strong connections between Jupiter and the other personal planets are inclined to give off a naturally upbeat aura, which creates a positive link to the process of attraction and manifestation.

Ticking boxes for the ego through working the Law of Attraction might not, however, be the highest use of Jupiter's power. On a soul level we will have signed up for particular experiences, and having material things delivered to us as if the Law of Attraction is another form of Amazon Prime isn't how the soul works. We know the soul's journey is far more complex than clicking our fingers and magicking up what the ego wants. In fact, the biggest cosmic joke – and blessing – can be the experience of *not* getting what we want! True abundance is a soul quality – and much more wonderful than any amount of money or material possessions.

 The greatest abundance we can have is to live without fear, expectation or attachment.

This is mastery and spiritual evolution.

Way Too Much – Jupiter as Maxed Out

Jupiter knows no boundaries, so wherever it is placed, we need to balance its exuberance with a sense of responsibility. Its tendency towards excess, risk-taking, being maxed out and over the top means it's easy to get careless and carried away. Larger than life, Jupiter can overdo everything and expect everything for nothing – let the freebies, goodie bags, air miles and good times permanently roll!

Jupiter's Outreach Policy – Distance in Miles and Meaning

 Jupiter's energy is not just about the making of money, but the making of meaning.

The position of Jupiter in the chart shows where we find pleasure and entertainment, but this is also a planet of wisdom. It shows our relationship to what we consider to be greater than the mundane. Tuning in to Jupiter enables us to look beyond what's physically evident to find greater meaning. How might we engage with the big questions and answers and the meaning of life?

Learning, further study, cultural pursuits and developing a spiritual philosophy are all part of Jupiter's imprint. It's also very much associated with travel, far horizons and distant locations. With a strongly placed Jupiter, you will get bored with what's inside your postcode! You might even be a globetrotter, cultural nomad and explorer of all the world has to offer. Your spiritual home might lie very far away...

Kindness and Gratitude – Jupiter's Generosity

Kindness is a state of spiritual awareness. Our light shines more brightly when we are kind to others. Even the simplest acts of kindness are a huge opening to high-frequency energy.

There is the Jupiter type who is the life and soul of the party – the *bon viveur* who makes people laugh and is the catalyst for good times. Then there is the Jupiter energy that radiates out energetically as an uplifting spirit, focusing on the positives, neutralizing problems and helping others widen their perspective and gain better outcomes. Channelling Jupiter's energy in the form of being kind and generous-spirited towards others raises the vibration for everyone and is a natural magnetic force for good.

> **Gratitude and appreciation are hugely connected to Jupiter's benevolence.**

Being grateful for blessings both big and small on a daily basis is well known to change your whole interaction with the seen and the unseen in a positive way. Being appreciative or able to spot the silver lining in the cloud is a vital act of intention designed to overcome difficulties and bring healing.

Jupiter's Potential

> **Jupiter's sign says a lot about what we have to offer and what we attract.**

Explore the potential of your own Jupiter's sign and discover where you have an abundance of positive energy that you can tap into in order to up-level your life.

Jupiter in Aries ♈

Full of daring, Jupiter in the sign of the ram is naturally heroic! Zeus's vantage point as the sky god propels you straight into the fast lane, ramping up your desire to achieve and do more. Of course, this is bound to create impulsive moves and this placement can make you a risk-taker and thrill-seeker. As Aries is such a me-first sign, Jupiter can magnify the more selfish and competitive tendencies too. But your mantra could be 'Fortune favours the bold!'

Tempered by more grounded energy, you are a positive entrepreneur who will stop at nothing to set a goal in motion. Yet that fieriness is usually generous-spirited and literally steps in where angels fear to tread to provide just what is required in the hour of need. You are the person who performs random acts of kindness or champions a cause or a person.

When you channel your Jupiter in Aries, you believe in manifesting your lucky breaks through sheer acts of will. You also adore a challenge that tests all your powers of strength, the harder the better. As a mentor, you will encourage someone to keep fighting on, urging them to be strong-minded and to take the upper hand.

Greatest Gift: Courage.
Up-levelling Jupiter: Dare to do your own thing.

Jupiter in Taurus ♉

Possessing the planet of plenty in the sign that is most associated with the sensory pleasures is guaranteed to give you a special affinity with the body and the material plane. You could call it the Midas touch or Jupiter in Taurus; either way, you just can't help being a magnet for money and all that it brings. Equally, you enjoy the pleasure of spending it — kind of rolling around in it — whenever possible. However, sometimes this Jupiter placement brings out the hoarder and the accumulator energy that gets you caught up in attachment to the big zeroes in the bank account.

You do like to have and to own, as this represents all that is solid and secure to you, so you are likely to have more than a few prized possessions. Given the phenomenal staying power of Taurus, these are destined to last a lifetime. A generous spirit, you can help others make money, too, or gift them with things. You do like to see people enjoying themselves.

In the realm of the body, Jupiter can imprint his largesse in size. The pleasures of the flesh are of course on your joy list. This also includes indulging in the delights of food that is not necessarily healthy but satisfies your gourmet inclinations. Think high-end restaurants and party-givers.

Greatest Gift: Pure enjoyment of the physical realm.
Up-levelling Jupiter: Become an architect of stability.

Jupiter in Gemini ♊

Jupiter's presence in this quick-witted sign bestows high-speed connection in the world of ideas and communication. Your mind races at a million miles per hour. Your gift of the gab allows you to discuss literally any topic and you're a mine of information that enables you to entertain others with dazzling repartee. You also move around a lot. You resonate with the butterfly energy of Gemini and dislike staying in one place for long, whilst Jupiter increases your curiosity in life and people.

What you are able to give others is exactly the right piece of information at exactly the right time. You can spin ideas that offer a myriad of new angles to a person who has got stuck. You're versatile, adaptable and blooming marvellous when it comes to people skills! You instinctively know who needs to meet whom and actively enjoy getting people together. As a mentor, you're a great facilitator, unless Jupiter's magnitude has focused you on being a collector of people for yourself.

Greatest Gift: Knowing everything and everyone!
Up-levelling Jupiter: Connect people and ideas and enable them to flow.

Jupiter in Cancer ♋

There is no one more adept at making you feel at home than someone with Jupiter in Cancer. You're so naturally relaxed and reassuring, you could even persuade someone that sitting on a minefield would be totally within their comfort zone! You like to take care of others and are so naturally empathetic that people absolutely know that you can read their mind as well as their tea leaves.

As Cancer is the sign of the family, Jupiter here can make the family a big deal, or a large one, or the vastness may be translated into the actual home itself. However it manifests, you enjoy creating the kind of atmosphere where everyone else feels your place is a home from home.

Your soothing presence and emotional intelligence are also nectar for the needy types who receive something of the divine mother or father from you. You have a knack of making people feel they are one of the family. Your tribal streak extends beyond blood ties and forms connections through emotional bonds rather than exclusively through DNA. You know how to enhance people, properties and emotional security.

Greatest Gift: Bonding.
Up-levelling Jupiter: Come from a place of empathy that allows grace to flow.

Jupiter in Leo ♌

When the planet of bigger and better lines up in the sign of magnificence, you are good at putting on a show! You have a natural capacity to express yourself, perform, draw attention and create a spectacle. You like to live life large – the royal sign of Leo can be quite flashy and definitely enjoys the luxuries in life. Yet Leo is also a generous sign, and with Jupiter there, you have a lot to give others. Sometimes this is in the less tangible realm of attention and kindness, but often it comes in the form of special treats that make a big difference and create a wow-factor.

Jupiter enables your natural radiance to shine through, which can help the Sun to come out in other people's lives. Yet when turned in on itself, it can be selfish, self-centred and egotistical. You can have an excessive streak that is born out of not knowing when to stop and not realizing that it is okay to be ordinary.

Nevertheless, you can make things sparkle for other people or add fire and warmth to someone's life. Your grand style is purely theatre – a means of adding colour and fun to the business of being human.

Greatest Gift: A big heart.
Up-levelling Jupiter: Tune in to the heartbeat of the greater good.

....

Jupiter in Virgo ♍

Jupiter's expansive properties aren't able to express themselves easily in the minimalist sign of Virgo. They don't fit comfortably, with Jupiter wishing to stretch and Virgo wishing to stay perfectly small. It's an interesting one for you, this natural push and pull, yet there are indeed ways in which the energies can fit happily together.

Virgo's natural affinity with the Earth, the wellbeing of the body and the smooth running of all things sets the stage for the planet that will do its level best to *be* the best in mind, body and spirit! So, you are the health freak, the dietary specialist and nutritionist. Also the admin person, fixer and organizer who can pull everything together for everyone.

Whilst Jupiter might overdo the more fretful side of Virgo's nature and encourage you to imagine worst-case scenarios, you will always be prepared with contingency plans. What you lack in spontaneity, you compensate for in sheer organizational skills. You can be generous with these also, advising others with your professional knowledge and eye for detail. You have practical life skills to offer and know what makes the world go round. What's more, you can make it happen.

Greatest Gift: Know-how.
Up-levelling Jupiter: Give yourself to helping others.

Jupiter in Libra ♎

Having the great benefic in Libra, the sign of relationships, is obviously a bonus when it comes to dealing with people, being able to bring out the best in them and developing excellent social skills. Jupiter here gives a huge amount of diplomacy and the capacity to negotiate, compromise and cooperate with others. This is best seen on a one-to-one basis, as you adapt to what is required in a relationship, deftly balancing what the other person wants with your own needs.

You naturally attract people to you and no matter where other planets are placed, you exert a kind of gravitational pull in the realm of relationships. You're also generous-spirited towards others and able to magnetize the right relationships.

You're a people person, essentially, and your talents extend towards solving relationship issues and neutralizing differences whilst maximizing the plus points of any partnership with ease and grace. You're inherently fair-minded and stand up for those who have not received what should rightfully be theirs. Relationships can be a source of great joy and personal growth for you, and the mutual exchange can offer much in terms of opening up wider horizons both culturally and socially.

Greatest Gift: Sharing.
Up-levelling Jupiter: Be peaceful and neutral in your dealings.

....

Jupiter in Scorpio ♏

Jupiter's riches turn to inner gold in the sign of Scorpio, if you are willing to work on yourself and to understand the profound truths about life and human nature. That is not to say that the material realm is lacking with Jupiter in Scorpio, as lead can be turned into gold in more visible form too.

Jupiter acts on a vast scale, so you can trawl through the very darkest areas and penetrate the depths of the human psyche, entering the shadow realm to engage with whatever is considered toxic, corrupt or dangerous to the world or an individual. You can also operate at a very light, bright level – you have the capacity to embrace extremes and be a great healer.

The intuition and perception of Scorpio makes Jupiter's presence here even more powerful. You need to use resources wisely, to employ your insight to help rather than harm and to emerge from your dealings with your integrity intact. As a mentor, you can bring others through crisis to transformation. Profound personal evolution is part of your journey.

Greatest Gift: Perception.
Up-levelling Jupiter: Give others your insights for healing and transformation.

Jupiter in Sagittarius ♐

Jupiter is in home territory in Sagittarius, as this planet is the ruler of this sign. Generating way too much of everything! You can be completely over the top with your sense of adventure and desire to explore everywhere and everything. If you never grow out of your party-animal phase, then your life can be endless hedonism. However, the true quest of both Jupiter and Sagittarius is to find meaning, to explore what's possible via travel, study or the school of life, in terms of human understanding.

The playful side of the archer extends to how you put your knowledge across. You can be a tease, a joker, but have a natural way of engaging people's interest. Really, you want to encourage others to push their own boundaries and discover all the possibilities in life. This can be a real gift. You feel you are fortunate and you can help others to find their own lucky star too.

Greatest Gift: Optimism.
Up-levelling Jupiter: Shine the light of your positivity into the world.

....

Jupiter in Capricorn ♑

The positive Jupiter and the cautious, hard-working Capricorn are a wise combination, favouring financial growth coupled with personal responsibility. At the very least this Jupiter placement suggests you have a good head for business and can spot an opportunity and apply yourself to making it real.

What you have to offer others is a serious and professional mindset, perhaps business acumen or possibly financial resources. Whatever you offer is likely to have been earned, rather than handed to you on a plate, so it is actually your experience that is of most value. You overcome adversity with a positive outlook and an eye for opportunity that is astute rather than reckless.

Whilst you yearn to achieve security, you're wise enough to know that it comes in many forms and that assets alone are not enough. Material success may represent your mountain peak, yet you appreciate the personal value of the challenge too. As a mentor, you can offer wise counsel that grounds others and shows them resilience is key.

Greatest Gift: Commitment.
Up-levelling Jupiter: Be a sustaining force for others and the world.

....

Jupiter in Aquarius ♒

You are the big networker and people carrier! It's almost as if you can see into the whole matrix that connects people and can create threads that group people together. You are a social creature, always wanting to be part of something and therefore working well within large organizations or communities. Ultimately, as Aquarius is so far-sighted, Jupiter here can see you pulling people together for the common good, whether it's with a gift for IT or humanitarian services!

This placement was made for the digital age. A facility for social media is at your fingertips and you can create large gatherings and platforms. Whether on- or offline, you find the thing that people have in common. As a mentor, you encourage people to think outside the box, as your ideas are often ingenious rather than mainstream.

Friendship is massively life-enhancing for you and you will be reaching far and wide into all walks of life, enjoying the company of others and making new friends of any age, at any age! However old you are, your curiosity about the new keeps you very current.

Greatest Gift: Openness.
Uplevelling Jupiter: Share your vision for helping people.

....

Jupiter in Pisces ♓

Easily able to tap into the mystical, creative, otherworldly realm of life, you have an affinity with all that is magical, romantic, atmospheric and soulful. No matter what other planetary placements you have in your chart, you will have an aura of sensitivity and empathy that offers emotional intelligence. Sometimes this is most readily expressed in the artistic and creative side of life. Certainly you appreciate the subtle effects that tend to pass others by.

You also have more than a hint of telepathy or psychic intuition that enables you to see beyond the veil, or at least into how anyone may be feeling at any moment. Therefore you have a gift for soothing hurt feelings and offering hope, inspiration and emotional support. The downside is that you may pick up too much, being a sponge for all that is circulating in the atmosphere, or even give too much, and from time to time need to heal yourself rather than being constantly plugged into others' needs. Staying balanced and grounded is as important as maintaining your connection to the divine.

Greatest Gift: Giving.
Up-levelling Jupiter: Radiate your mystical force for healing.

Aspects to the Personal Planets

Take a look at your birth chart to see how Jupiter fits into the overall picture with your other planets. What aspects do you have between Jupiter and your personal planets? When you see how Jupiter fits with other planetary patterns of who you are meant to become, you'll get an idea as to whether it's a *crescendo* or *pianissimo* vibration in your life.

Jupiter–Sun

Aspects between high-vibe Jupiter and the Sun generate a real sense of being a positive influencer. There's a need to explore other cultures, travel, learn, have fun, keep growing and developing, and also the provision of positive energy that keeps others afloat. In many ways, Jupiter's larger-than-life energy translates quite literally into living a high-impact, big life. Your generous spirit combines with warmth, optimism and the desire to live life to the full. You tend to have a 'lucky' streak. That simply means that you find it relatively easy to plug into the Law of Attraction.

Jupiter–Moon

When you find Jupiter in aspect to the Moon, your personal and emotional life is coloured by effusive Jupiter, creating vivid experiences. You tend to be philosophical, caring and giving, and your soul path inclines you to look after others and support them with your optimistic outlook and protection. Your own home might be a true place of sanctuary and respite, or perhaps a place where others are entertained. Waking up to the spiritually meaningful side of life is a great source of comfort to you.

Jupiter–Mercury

Jupiter's expansive energy floods Mercury, the planet of the mind, with an endless stream of ideas. It's difficult for you to stand still, because you're always looking to see how things could develop. Being a natural communicator, teacher or marketeer, you know how to make things sound appealing and your enthusiasm is infectious. You could be a motivational speaker, a life coach or an entrepreneur, as you thrive on having an outlet for spreading knowledge and uplift. Your soul seeks to learn, whilst your mind thirsts for ever-widening horizons.

Jupiter–Venus

The engaging combination of Jupiter and Venus infuses you with a warm personal approach which draws people to you. Here the openness of Jupiter serves to optimize relationships, producing a wide network of friends and opportunities for relationship. You magnetize people from different cultural backgrounds and love to travel. Entertainment, socializing, pleasure, love and the arts are likely to be big players in your life story and your generous spirit is given freely, enhancing other people's lives.

Jupiter–Mars

The ever-exuberant frequency of Jupiter pulses together with Mars to keep pushing forward. When these planets combine their go-getting energies, there's no sense of there being barriers to what's possible. Yet all this enthusiasm can lead to over-extension if not countered with common sense and groundedness. Still, your playful, positive approach lights other people up and helps to promote goodwill. You are an adventurer, an irrepressible force of nature who is always seeking, searching and moving towards new goals.

CHAPTER 10

Saturn

Karma, hard work, self-discipline, commitment

How can I meet my challenges?
What are my life's lessons?

Saturn (♄ in your chart) is the work we need to do. Yes, good old Saturn is the planet of hard work and applying ourselves to the task in hand. It's often associated with immersing ourselves in the grind of life, undertaking serious studies or responsibilities in order to improve or prove ourselves.

 Saturn gives us the intent to manifest.

Its energy ensures we are grounded, self-disciplined and capable of being productive and constructive. It triggers us to ask ourselves if we've got what it takes to do a good job.

Saturn is the planet of plans. We all need a working strategy for life that gives us something to strive for. This may be in any sphere, but is usually connected to what we believe will give us security and stability.

Saturn is also our default setting for getting through. It requires us to focus and concentrate in order to 'pass the test', which might be an academic requirement or a lesson from the school of life. Understandably, Saturn gets a bad rap when it comes to restricting pleasure and being no fun at all. Yet without Saturn, we might not learn anything very much. We might not strive to do our best, to prove ourselves. It is, after all, the planet of excellence, achievement and accomplishment, which will be a reward for our efforts, not something that lands in our lap. It can be said that sometimes hugely important lessons are learned from failure too. It is the undertaking of the task, the experience of being put to the test, that is important for the soul, rather than success in earthly terms.

It's Karma!

Saturn has a reputation for being the Lord of Karma, the planet that presides over our soul contract, our slice of life, our actions and their consequences.

 What is karma? The idea that for every action there is a reaction.

What goes around comes around, you reap what you sow, cause and effect – for thousands of years humanity has played with the idea of morality or good deeds generating rewards, whereas bad deeds or even thoughts create a negative loop.

For the purposes of astrology, the retribution or reward scenario isn't about the judgement of a god, but the lessons to be learned by the evolving soul. Since good things happen to bad people and the other way around, we can't always make sense of, much less understand, our karma as being the results of our previous actions. Most probably, the karma experience is far more complex than we can consciously compute.

Saturn is the orchestrator of our karma and its position in our chart gives us clues as to what we need to learn or the balance we need to redress. So, if Saturn is the planet of our unfinished business, how do we finish it? Can we detach from our karmic involvements and limited patterns? Might it be possible to collapse our karma?

Taking responsibility for what happens, whether it has been 'done' to us or not, is a major step forward.

> ***The idea of having chosen to experience a lesson is absolutely empowering and halts the victim mentality and the blame culture.***

If everything happens for a reason, it's possible that Saturn is a way to understand that reason. Saturn asks us to face things and either do something about them or accept them and make the choice to move on.

It's not that Saturn is asking us to live the life of a saint. Just to think about the consequences of everything we do, the effect we are having on others, on our environment, the mark we are leaving, the stain on our soul records, and any wounds that have been inflicted on others.

The concept of karma includes the karma of deeds, words, thoughts, even the karma of association!

We may get instant karma, which presents pretty immediately in an obvious way to us, or the reactions to our actions may lie dormant and we may remain oblivious to them. Until next time around. As they say, ignorance is bliss. But not any more! Remaining passive, not addressing Saturn and our karmic footprint, and not being accountable just means that we are going to have to look at the issue again at some point.

Ultimately, some form of enlightenment comes from basing decisions on the law of least karma. Meaning travelling lightly so that we aren't making waves, or ripples, that will need to be dealt with at a later date.

The Ties That Bind Us to Others

Ever since ancient astrologers first gazed at Saturn, it has been known as the Lord of Time. It governs the timing of cycles, events and meetings.

Saturn is like the grammar of life, the punctuation mark that defines where we are in the narrative of our life story.

In terms of karma, Saturn presides over endings and beginnings – the point when something is over or when we enter into a commitment.

On the Earth plane, we can get stuck into a relationship or a project and apply ourselves to making progress, both spiritually and in earthly terms, but things can move slowly. Saturn enables us to go into things for the long haul. For as long as it takes. We use terms such as our 'forever house' or 'forever relationship', yet Saturn is the energy that binds or severs the contract. Cuts the cords if need be, if the karma is over or there is something elsewhere that needs to be learned.

> ### Saturn contains the glue that
> ### creates our attachments.

It is associated with the capacity to hold on, in terms of making relationships or roles last. It is planet permanence! We ring-fence what we wish to protect with Saturn, the planet that has its own rings around itself. We may indeed choose to wear a ring that marks us as exclusive to another person. Saturn is about the creation of boundaries, protocols for controlling the more primitive instincts – both ours and other people's! Yet its energy is present in separation too, when there is a serious knowing that something is over.

Yet we don't always conform to Saturn's protocols – we break the rules, the contract or the agreement. We all have free will, which we use to navigate our lives, sometimes making choices that resonate with our soul's plan of who we came here to be, sometimes not. Whatever choices we make, ultimately our desires could cost us in the future if they don't resonate with the highest good.

Why We Hold Back – Saturn in Control

When it comes to feelings, Saturn is inextricably linked with their repression rather than expression. It is there when we are operating in survival mode, out of duty, practicality or responsibility rather than living from the heart. This may have been learned from an early age, as part of our emotional conditioning and pattern. Withholding our feelings can be seen as a sign of early maturity and self-control. So, from a young age we may stuff our feelings down and develop a hard defence mechanism. As an adult, we may consider this shutting down as compliance with the family dynamic and not the healthiest way to maintain a connected relationship with others. Sooner or later we may yearn to lower our defences and experience the vulnerability of a heartfelt, trusting, emotional connection.

Whichever way we relate to Saturn, it always asks us to contain ourselves. Sometimes this becomes so acute – the need for approval or success becomes so strong – that we deny our needs and instincts. A coldness sets in, we close down, are less available to others and to our true selves. We spend our lives managing the external, material realm, paying little attention to what is really going on at an emotional level. Are we self-sufficient or shut down? Saturn's tight boundaries can leave us isolated, alone and disconnected. Ideally, we need to find a balance between being a mature, wise adult and retaining our capacity to truly connect on a heart and soul level.

Transforming the Core Wound into a Core Strength

Saturn's presence can highlight where we feel 'less than', insecure or inhibited. Saturn pinpoints our core wound. We can feel hurt here, or inadequate. It's a sensitive spot. But it's actually our training ground! It's possible to harness Saturn's energy in order to grow, to fill in the lack, to right the wrong. We can build on this, overcome it, become wise about it.

*The minute we take responsibility for
our healing, the magic begins.*

Saturn is necessarily slow, so there are no quick fixes, but this is part of the beauty of creating something solid. With patience and perseverance, we get to be an expert on the matters associated with our self-perceived 'flaw', turning the wound into substantial wisdom that is a foundation of our life and a valuable resource for others who are struggling.

Saturn's Great Reality Check

As the planet that deals with straight facts and figures, Saturn brings us down to earth. It is very much the energy of the material plane, earthly reality. This is a frequency of common sense and logic, instead of imagination and intuition. With Saturn, it is a case of 'needs must' rather than wishes and fantasies.

This can feel rather stark and bleak, but Saturn is what it is and it teaches us to be what and where we are – to anchor ourselves in the physical realm. To be rooted in the tangible plane of reality.

 The reality of Saturn is also a comfort zone that helps us know where we stand.

Integrating Saturn gives our life shape and definition; we learn to manage chaos through organization and clear thinking. With Saturn, there's no shirking the mundane business and boring bits, no matter how much we might wish to fly around on the astral plane or in our dream world. But this is valuable. We all need to know how to live within the confines of the human body and to have our feet on the ground.

Transits of Saturn

From the age of seven onwards, every seven years Saturn will form an angle to our Saturn placement. The proverbial seven-year itch, seven-year cycles and multiples thereof can mark an opt-in or opt-out clause in our karma, releasing us from, renewing or establishing bonds. Obviously it works best when we can approach these points with a full capacity to let go of what is tired and outgrown, no longer fit for purpose. Clearing space energetically – both physically and emotionally – is an ongoing process of taking responsibility for how we live. A Saturn transit can be a tough time, marking a period where less is more and we feel the need to cut back the surplus and focus on priorities. Yet Saturn can also bring the relief and reward of completion and achievement.

Saturn Returns

Our life span is encapsulated within the marker points of Saturn's cycles: 0–29, 30–59, 60–89, onwards.

The first Saturn return, at the age of 29, usually brings a demarcation line between the past and the future. At this point, big decisions are made, because Saturn has completed its first journey around our chart, met all our planets and initiated us into the grown-up awareness of all we can be. This is when we often feel called to leave behind our childhood, or even decisions made before the Saturn return that no longer resonate with the adult we wish to become. A rite of passage is an ending and beginning, a responsibility, such as a marriage, career or parenthood, which is the flag carrier for the next cycle. It marks the initial formation of the ego and carries the imprint of our soul lessons.

The second Saturn return, at the age of 59, occurs when we have completed our middle adult cycle and are looking at the third age. We may need to shed some of the accoutrements of our middle years, as we switch from accumulating to giving. As with the first Saturn return, it is a threshold crossing – the age of 60 marking our entry point into being a wise older person. A review of our achievements takes place. Our life lessons are plain to see. We can shift priorities to rebalance our energy and move into a whole different level of fulfilment and meaning.

Between 59 and 89 we take on the most senior cycle, until 89 ushers us into the age of the elder. Our physical body may not be what it used to be, but our legacies and learning become more obvious, and advice and guidance can be given to those in their younger cycles. We are becoming aware of the whole of our life journey, what it means, what we would like to leave behind, what really matters. This is Saturn's summing-up and gift to ourselves and others.

Saturn Creates the Diamond Soul

The sign occupied by Saturn reveals the specific soul lessons we have to work with and integrate for personal transformation. When we work with our destiny we become a beautiful and wise diamond soul.

Saturn in Aries ♈

With Saturn in Aries, your core fire must be burnished like steel in the furnace of life's tests and challenges. There is no other way. No one else can do it for you. Aries is a pioneer force, independent and courageous. No matter what other planetary placements you have, the universe is asking you to develop your capacity to do battle. Lessons may come in the form of self-reliance, and taking personal responsibility for working through your karma is important. But inside you is a fighting spirit – you have everything you need within you to work through that karma.

What We Fear: Failure.
Life Lesson: Self-actualization.
How to Take Control of Your Destiny: It's down to you!

Saturn in Taurus ♉

Learning how to manifest a level of security is a key challenge for you. Learning how to manifest money is one thing, learning how to keep hold of it is another. You are likely to experience tests in the material realm so that you become adept at handling material resources and things of a physical nature. Care of the body is important for you – a healthy relationship with nature and food. You also possess skills for the slow build and preservation of your security. Whilst abundance might be a goal, simplicity is your perfection.

What We Fear: Not having enough.
Life Lesson: Endurance.
How to Take Control of Your Destiny: With patience and practicality.

....

Saturn in Gemini ♊

When the super-quick processing powers of Gemini are brought together with Saturn's structure and wisdom, the big issue is how you relate to the mind. Is it your conduit to the world or your enslavement? Academic credentials could be sought as a means of bolstering self-esteem, rather than for the joy of learning itself. Whilst you can develop extraordinary logistical and analytical skills, excel at technology or as an expert in your field, your life lesson is to develop wisdom rather than knowledge.

What We Fear: Not knowing enough.
Life Lesson: Mastery includes both the head and the heart.
How to Take Control of Your Destiny: With an enquiring mind.

....

Saturn in Cancer ♋

Saturn brings lessons in self-defence for the soft-shelled crab – the need to protect yourself from emotional wounds requires a strong boundary between yourself and others. Saturn can require you to develop a huge level of maturity in the early years. Family responsibilities may loom large. Yet, providing you create a safe space for your own vulnerability, you can learn to be both emotionally connected and self-supporting – a valuable blueprint for healthy relationships.

What We Fear: Is it safe to open up?
Life Lesson: Developing emotional resilience.
How to Take Control of Your Destiny: With inner strength.

Saturn in Leo ♌

When stern Saturn is situated in the playfully expressive sign of Leo, a certain stage-fright can set in. There can be self-consciousness, shyness or a fear of showing off. But if Saturn shuts down some of the grandiosity of the big cat, it can also hone its solar fire into a true heart of gold. There's a dignity about you and a capacity to create with gravitas. Saturn's lessons in the humbling of the ego can result in true love emerging as a strength fuelled by inner warmth.

What We Fear: Lack of love.
Life Lesson: Love is an inside job.
How to Take Control of Your Destiny: With inner radiance.

Saturn in Virgo ♍

With Saturn in the perfectionist sign of Virgo, you have a super-sharp critical eye. You are in fact the expert on 'what could go wrong'. This works well if you have a job as a risk analyst, but in everyday life the negatives need to be put in perspective and set against the positives. You worry about contamination, which feeds into a health-conscious attitude, but operating at maximum tilt can veer into OCD or anxiety. However, your capacity for discernment is a tremendous life skill. You know where and when to cultivate and to discard.

What We Fear: Being out of control.
Life Lesson: Moving between quality control and letting go.
How to Take Control of Your Destiny: With reality checks.

....

Saturn in Libra ♎

Libra's innate sense of grace can be weighed down by Saturn's down-to-earth approach. You walk the tightrope between the ugly business and the beautifully formed. However, with Saturn here, you can be the ultimate in seeing what is fair and just, working towards resolving differences or legal settlements. You consider beauty and the arts a serious business and value them highly. The art of relationship is another of your skills, with Saturn ensuring you can offer good counsel and negotiating skills both personally and professionally.

What We Fear: Inequality.

Life Lesson: Everything is relative.

How to Take Control of Your Destiny: With good grace and social skills.

....

Saturn in Scorpio ♏

Saturn in the most undercover sign of them all indicates some of the most important things in your life are kept hidden. There's bound to be a lot teeming beneath the surface in your life. You have an eagle-eyed capacity to discover what makes others tick, or to dig up the dirt. People reveal themselves to you, but you will only reciprocate if you feel totally safe. There are psychological riches underneath, which is your passport to a great level of awareness and understanding.

What We Fear: That others will control you.

Life Lesson: Repression leads to stagnation.

How to Take Control of Your Destiny: With superpowers of perception and transformation.

....

Saturn in Sagittarius ♐

Saturn in the questing sign of Sagittarius suggests a big connection with faraway places and/or some kind of big deal around the pursuit of knowledge. Perpetual student or traveller, you search and seek. It is likely that you prefer the journey rather than the destination, the pursuit rather than the attainment of knowledge as Sagittarius is always opening up to new realms and possibilities. Stepping up to the role of mentor rather than adventurer is a sign that you have achieved a level of meaning that can guide others. Lessons can come about through risks taken and Saturn's mission is to curb your excesses.

What We Fear: Missing out.
Life Lesson: Learning from mistakes.
How to Take Control of Your Destiny: With optimism.

Saturn in Capricorn ♑

Saturn in its ruling sign can feel somewhat repressive, as a need to be responsible hovers over you from an early age. Hard work is how you achieve your goals. You may be defensive rather than carefree, yet the pay-off is security, however you measure it. You may be so hierarchical in nature that you are consumed by climbing the rungs of the success ladder. Top jobs lie at the top of your mountain and material resources are stashed away as a prize. Yet inner self-worth will be an issue, so the best work you can do is on yourself!

What We Fear: Losing it.
Life Lesson: Control is a defence.
How to Take Control of Your Destiny: With effort, dedication and self-discipline.

Saturn in Aquarius ♒

Saturn in the sign of friendship can make you a networker or outsider. You can switch between both, as change is no problem for you. Rules could be a problem, however, as your natural tendency is to buck them and start a revolution. This could be your training ground from school through work and result in you honing your individual and original style. Being radical or counter-cultural is a release for you, yet there always seems to be something that draws you into the mainstream in order to shake it up.

What We Fear: Being 'normal'.
Life Lesson: To be part of the whole yet detached.
How to Take Control of Your Destiny: In your own way.

Saturn in Pisces ♓

Order meets chaos – structured Saturn in the fluid world of Pisces presents an interesting conundrum. This is the classic control versus flow polarity, yet you've got them both and must find a way to make it work! If you're not too hard on yourself then you can become a professional creative, a person who is both grounded and otherworldly, combining head and heart, a professional healer. There are all manner of ways in which this placement can be expressed. Yet the big issue is always the handling of the material, mundane world whilst still retaining that visionary, numinous quality in your life.

What We Fear: Loss.

Life Lesson: To combine heaven and Earth.

How to Take Control of Your Destiny: With perspiration and inspiration!

Aspects to the Personal Planets

Take a look at your birth chart to see how Saturn fits into the overall picture with your other planets. When it is in aspect with your Sun, Moon, Mercury, Venus or Mars, you'll be carrying its vibration in a noticeable way. It will be a dominant influence – with its lessons clearly laid out and repeated for your personal growth.

Saturn–Sun

When Saturn is tied into the Sun by aspect, you have a special assignment in terms of personal development. There's an added weight to your life story, requiring you to focus and develop a sense of self-responsibility. Most importantly, to find that vital sense of self. Sun–Saturn aspects confer maturity from a young age. The need to prove yourself means you believe you should work harder and try harder than others. You are serious about getting things right. Applying yourself to the tasks of your life creates a sense of achievement – even if it's initially driven by an unconscious question mark over whether you feel good enough. You bring about a remarkable breakthrough when you develop a sense of self-worth and when you relax instead of control.

Saturn–Moon

If Saturn influences the Moon, you tend to take on extra responsibilities for home and family. Your soul lesson involves staying emotionally and personally strong and you learn to contain your feelings and find a way to make things work. This practical approach can appear emotionally defended, yet you simply believe in relying on yourself and in using your strength as a support for others. You believe in reliability and permanence, practicality rather than idealism. Your soul mission is to create emotional security. Being shy or contained is your way of staying safe and you tend to prefer a conventional path rather than veering off-*piste*. Attaining inner resilience means you become a role model for others who are needier, yet letting others in is important for preventing isolation.

Saturn–Mercury

Saturn's aspects to Mercury offer a practical, well-put-together thought process. You're unlikely to either jump to conclusions or veer too far off the path of the tried and tested. Saturn works hard in the area of the mind, developing a steady, methodical and thorough approach. You prefer to focus and concentrate rather than improvise both in conversation and thought. Becoming an expert can appeal to you, and once something is learned, you tend to retain the knowledge. Sometimes this placement leads to narrow thinking or to being overly serious. Which of course can be overcome with self-awareness.

Saturn–Venus

With these aspects, your Venus vibe is tempered by Saturn's desire for things to be real rather than illusory. Therefore you have great discernment in relationships and know how to put boundaries in place as a safety precaution. Karma and relationships go together with this placement, attracting those with whom you have soul contracts and unfinished business. You won't dally with meaningless relationships and your love frequency tends to be serious, committed and loyal. You value security and your love lessons involve building your own self-worth and self-love. You have the staying power to form lasting relationships that involve working through challenges. Opening your heart requires you to trust and relax into love.

Saturn–Mars

Saturn is slow and skilful rather than impulsive and upfront. So, you're the kind of person who applies yourself and possesses powers of endurance and resilience. You need to develop confidence, yet you have an enormous capacity to work your way through various tests and challenges. You have an ordered and controlled approach towards what you undertake, strategizing, focusing and working towards rather than 'giving things a go'. Your soul frequency is slow and steady, with a desire to achieve goals and earn rewards through effort.

Part IV

The Outer Planets

Uranus, Neptune and Pluto are known as the outer or transpersonal planets. They are further away from the Earth in our solar system and move much more slowly than, say, the Moon, which spends two and a half days in each sign every month. Uranus stays in a sign for approximately seven years, Neptune 14 years, Pluto between 12 and 21 years. Therefore, the sign position of these outer planets is less personal. It signals the generational wave of energy into which we are born. Our peer group will be part of this bubble of collective consciousness, a soul group invested in a particular social and collective awareness.

Uranus, Neptune and Pluto will be positioned in the sign of your generational wave and placed in one of the 12 houses according to your time of birth. Check the house diagram (*on page 22*) to find out in which areas of life your outer planets are positioned. It is within these settings that their energies will be active.

Next, look at your birth chart to see what matches your personal planets (Sun, Moon, Mercury, Venus and Mars) make with your outer planets. Look to see if there's a conjunction, sextile, trine, square or opposition between them. These indicate you have a strong frequency match with this outer planet. It's part of your plan in terms of who you came here to be! If you have no personal aspects to a particular outer planet, you may be less drawn into its vibration, experiencing it mainly through its house placement.

With the harmonious sextile or trine aspects, you are likely to be able to integrate these energies into your life readily and easily. You can flow with their meaning and purpose.

With the more challenging conjunction, square or opposition, there is work to be done, which may involve radical changes on your part. These soul codes indicate the need to wake up to these energies and transform yourself through experiencing their less conscious expression and up-levelling to their highest vibration. In this way you are unlocking your full cosmic potential.

With any major aspect between your personal and the outer planets, you have the specific soul intention to embody and live these energies as consciously as possible and use them to raise your frequency, wisdom and awareness.

 These aspects enable you to take control of your destiny!

CHAPTER 11

Uranus

*Wow-factor, radical change,
independence, innovation*

How can I make a difference?
Where am I radical? Where do I stand out?

As a planet, Uranus (♅ in your chart) carries the blueprint of radical, revolutionary energy. Wherever it is positioned in our chart, we will need to up-level from the ordinary to the extraordinary. This can occur through circumstances beyond our control, or through desiring to break away from old patterns and conditions.

 **Freedom, truth and independence are
the soul signatures of Uranus.**

We're a true Uranian type if we're an awakener, a free spirit, someone who feels 'different' from the accepted norm. Uranus pulses with electrical energy that lights up our unique path – a path that often takes us in a very different direction from our roots, cohorts, peer group and those close to us.

The opposite energy pattern to radical Uranus is compliance and conformity. We may fit in because we don't want to be an outsider, to make waves, to disrupt the status quo. Living our truth isn't always an easy ride. It means standing out from the crowd and attracting pushback for living or thinking differently and daring to be unique. Polarities always create tension, so there may be a case for internally aligning with what's true for us, rather than always taking the road less travelled. The planets all have their message, their call, and like an orchestral conductor, we need to arrange who plays when and create a symphony of self-expression, rather than having one planet hogging all the airtime!

Excitement on the Edge of Change

Uranus is the kind of energy that comes out of nowhere, bowls us over and takes us by surprise. This planet acts swiftly to turn things upside down, to alter the set-up and take us in a new direction. Not for nothing is it known as the planet of change.

 When Uranus is active, we simply can't keep things the same.

We find ourselves caught up in revolutionary energy, whether we're the perpetrator or on the receiving end. It can feel really thrilling when something happens out of the blue, or it can feel shockingly like the security and stability of the known is at stake. Either way, the excitement that accompanies Uranus keeps us on the edge of our seat.

The Awakener

With Uranus energy it's impossible to put the genie back in the bottle. Once unleashed, once glimpsed, we cannot un-see it. This is why Uranus is known as the awakener and game-changer. It literally alters what's possible – sometimes by bringing what we never thought would happen.

This is the planet that reveals new pathways, helping us change tack, alter course and leave the past behind. What used to be our comfort zone can seem suffocating when Uranus offers liberation. We begin to sense a brilliant new departure will give us a new lease of life. In certain circumstances we can finally become our own person.

 New dimensions and energies come into our life.

Disrupter Energy

If we aren't able to get hold of and live out our Uranus energy, we're likely to unconsciously invite it to come into our life from the outside. This is known as 'projection' in psychology-speak. In this case, it means the status quo is going to get stirred up. Perhaps we haven't felt entirely happy in a relationship, but it's our partner who leaves, embodying the Uranian disruptive force and bringing a mixture of trauma and relief. Or maybe a job ends without warning, but once we've got over the shock, we find greater fulfilment in a different setting.

However it happens, Uranus shakes things up and demands that we explore other options. This can be a creative change in the long run, even if we feel an outward level of security has been sacrificed.

Uranus is a catalyst for growth.

Also, as everything in this life is temporary, Uranus does a good job of alerting us all to the law of impermanence. Being able to move with the times and embrace the new is a way of making friends with the concept that all things must pass.

Breakthrough to the Unlived Life

Our chart holds the secret messages of all our life and personal growth potential, some of which we don't live or we consign to unconsciousness. We may be creative, for example, but this lies dormant as we get on with the day job. We might have a restless spirit, but societal norms say settling down is the right thing to do.

Strong Uranus aspects to our personal planets may not operate 24/7 in everyday life, but the soul intention is that Uranus must be included somewhere, so there's wiggle room for the new to come in. By transit, this planet can literally appear like a lightning bolt.

When Uranus is highly active in our chart, with inner planets making strong aspects to its electrical sparks, or it comes along by transit as a wake-up call, we get to experience life on a radically different frequency. Its energy serves to remove the old without warning and clear out stuck patterns.

A Uranus transit seems like a flash in the pan, a pop-up, something that doesn't last forever. But its purpose has been to show us how to live the unlived life. When the transit is gone and the flashpoint is over, new energy has been downloaded and integrated into the whole of our being.

Cut off and Detached

Uranus steps right outside the familiar need for attachment. Its frequency is primarily head- rather than heart-oriented. With its sudden sweeps, it encourages us to detach from all-consuming personal feelings.

 Uranus is the wild card that presses the 'refresh' button, rendering the old patterns null and void.

With Uranus, the soul message of who you are here to become is to dare to be yourself, rather than people-please. If you've always revolved around other people's needs, this can seem cut off from the heart and rather selfish. The flip side of Uranian-type behaviour can seem *too* detached – cutting off from emotional sensitivity and doing your own thing without any regard for how others might feel or the impact of your divergence from the status quo. Of course, there's a balance to be struck between being true to ourselves and not losing touch with the heart.

 Uranus can take us to a soul-level, Higher-Self perspective where there's awareness that our true essence is beyond identifying with either our fluctuating feelings or our thoughts.

Can we take a leap into detaching from the never-ending demands of our thoughts and feelings? Can we view what's going on without lowering our vibration into suffering, which is so often caused by our attachments?

The Wow-Factor

Wild-card Uranus doesn't want us to stagnate in our comfort zone, but to step outside of it and stretch ourselves to explore something new and different. This is the call of the soul to wrest itself from the small ego and align with the capacity to live in the present without expectations. Coming from this place is very liberating and ultimately means we will grow beyond the tiny ego mind into a hugely expansive perception that embraces change as personal evolution. The wow-factor of living in the present blows away the cobwebs of the past and expectations of the future and makes us 100 per cent available in the now!

 Living as our radically now self enables the vibration we emit to others to literally be the difference we seek!

Uranus Signature Signs

The Generational Wave

Uranus spends approximately seven years in each sign and takes 84 years to complete its circle of the zodiac. These are its areas of focus in each sign:

Uranus in Aries ♈
Seeking the self and rapid change.

Uranus in Taurus ♉
New ways of dealing with farming, finance and food.

Uranus in Gemini ♊
Communication and educational breakthroughs.

Uranus in Cancer ♋
Changes in property and family values.

Uranus in Leo ♌
Search for the self.

Uranus in Virgo ♍
Health and self-care breakthroughs.

Uranus in Libra ♎
Redefining relationship, design and beauty.

Uranus in Scorpio ♏
Research and discovery.

Uranus in Sagittarius ♐
Advances in travel, education and learning.

Uranus in Capricorn ♑
Challenges to the establishment.

Uranus in Aquarius ♒︎
Technological advances, new awareness.

Uranus in Pisces ♓︎
Visionary, humanitarian drives.

Aspects to the Personal Planets

Uranus–Sun

Put simply, you were never meant to be the same as other people! There is something about your soul plan that takes you on a different path. Your timing might be different, there may be less desire to fit in and you definitely need space to be yourself rather than conform to the rat-race mentality. Your career path and personal growth flourish with plenty of individual freedom. On the other hand, you are an innovator, so may bring new awareness, ideas or technological advances into the mainstream. The developmental path your soul intended is to be ahead of the curve, so it takes others a while to catch up with you. Your life story cuts through convention, showing people that it's possible to 'do it your way'. You're essentially a way-shower. You come in and out of people's lives to wake them up.

Uranus–Moon

As the Moon reveals your comfort zone and Uranus carries an electrifying frequency, it can be difficult for you to find that 'safe space', as things are shaken up or you're forced out of the nest in some way. As the Uranus–Moon patterns suggest disruption in childhood family life, you're used to keeping moving rather than settling in. Yet as Uranus is so erratic and intermittent, it's possible that you become entrenched for many years and then uprooted again, or you feel the need to satisfy your inner desire for emotional freedom. You have a restlessness within you that thirsts for excitement. 'Normal' doesn't appeal as much as creating your own version of what works for you. There's also a freshness and uniqueness about your personal energy field that radiates out to others. You crackle with personal magnetism that others find both attractive and challenging!

Uranus–Mercury

Your mind is wired up to the higher mind, so you're constantly being pulsed with ideas from another realm. Some of these may seem so abstract, ahead of their time or off the wall that it's difficult to land and manifest them. Your original thinking is genius, but can pose challenges in formal education. You're happiest in an environment that is progressive enough to value your unique input. Like electricity, you can find yourself in full flow and then experience a power cut – the mental thought forms tend to switch on and off. You can be super-quick on the uptake, grasping abstract concepts that pass others by. Yet your mental energy is restless and easily distracted, so it's hard to focus. Besides which, you tend to lose interest in anything repetitive or overly structured. On a soul level, you've definitely got an unusual message to offer that stimulates new neural pathways in others!

Uranus–Venus

When the wild planet Uranus aspects your natal Venus, it's bound to make interventions in your love life that spark diversions in the storyline! Uranus is the planet that corresponds to surprise, so inevitably relationships can begin or end suddenly. The more consciously aware you become of your Uranian need for excitement, the more you can keep the show on the road, whilst changing the scenery. In other words, your relationships become the catalysts and agents for personal growth rather than the recipients of unexpected eruptions. Your role as an awakener can have a startling impact on those in relationship with you. Or you may find yourself attracted to people who embody the Uranian energy of being very different from you or at odds with the mainstream. Together, you can switch things up. However, Uranus aspects to Venus do tend to have a 'rollercoaster' effect on relationships. An adrenaline spike is never far away!

Uranus–Mars

The sheer volatility and high-voltage energy of Uranus are very evident when it's in aspect to the personal drive of Mars. So, there's a revelatory, spontaneous frequency about you that is immediately apparent. You're the catalyst for introducing new ideas and have an affinity for anything out of the ordinary. Naturally able to deal with shifting circumstances, you thrive on stimulation that produces different challenges every day, though you're not so keen on being told what to do and how to do it. Your rebel energy fires you with enthusiasm to revolutionize the old ways and to maintain your personal space and freedom. Your soul path takes you down some unusual routes that enable you to make changes in your own life goals and alter the status quo with speed. You are something of a pop-up!

CHAPTER 12

Neptune

*Sensitivity, emotional intelligence,
intuition, creativity*

What is my dream?
How can I channel inspiration?

All planets are nuanced and multi-tonal, but perhaps none more so than Neptune (Ψ in your chart) – a planet that is often implicated when we feel in the depths of despair and again when we feel euphoric and blissful.

The magical dream world that is Neptune is more real to some people than to others. For empaths, star-seeds, creatives or sensitively wired or awakened souls, it is as accessible as the street outside. A 'Neptunian', i.e., someone attuned to Neptune, can channel inspiration from this otherworldly realm because they're used to dipping into it. It is the place where dreams are made, images are woven, healing is downloaded and transcendence and grace reside.

For other people, Neptune's subtleties lie uncomfortably far away from the everyday senses, the tangible, material world and *terra firma* that make up mundane reality. For those wedded to the material, tangible realm, it takes conscious awareness to open up to the fifth dimension and receive the inspiration available. But Neptune is totally quantum. It connects us all, unites us in a field of resonance – the very same one in which the Law of Attraction operates.

Neptune is the planet
that helps us to 'magic things up'.

It activates our wish-list. Yet we don't always get everything our ego wants.... Challenges to the attachments of the ego are part of Neptune's territory. These involve surrender and letting go of the personal ego in order to attain greater understanding and awareness. There is mystery and magic in discovering who we are here to become.

Accessing the Intuitive Realm

The linear mind is more closely aligned with rational thought and reasoning. Its limitation is that it deems the imaginative, intuitive realm 'unreasonable', lacking in gravitas and evidence. Yet it's the realm of intuition that connects us to the power of universal truth, rather than the tick-box answers of the scientific realm. When we can lift up into the higher mind and connect with our intuition, we're more likely to grasp the subtle truths and intuitive answers that are impossible to find at ground level. Yet Neptune makes them accessible.

Astrology itself, although it has an astronomical, scientific basis, is more aligned with Neptune's realm of intuition, mystery and awareness. The ego mind searches for clear-cut, right or wrong results, as it desires control, whereas Neptune's domain is that of understanding, reflection and enlightenment.

It is in Neptune's domain that we receive guidance both from our inner self and from Source. Sometimes dreams speak to us, or we literally 'channel' our insight. *We just know.*

Neptune's Healing Powers

When Neptune touches us, we are sensitized and in some instances made vulnerable or delicate. We are softened, we open up, we allow healing in, we connect with our feelings rather than our thoughts.

> **One of the greatest healings is to surrender to what is – and Neptune is the gateway planet to this kind of acceptance, forgiveness and letting go.**

The enormous relief we get from experiencing the healing power of Neptune is that we allow ourselves to move into the opposite of control. We stop having to 'do' things and just float or go with the flow. We can let things be. There is peace here. We reach a state of compassion for ourselves and others.

We can access another dimension – the divine, the spiritual – and a state of grace that transcends all the drama, the problems, the striving. We touch the soul here and have access to the wisdom of the spiritual realm. It's nothing short of a miracle.

Liars, Fakes and Suffering – the Flip Side of Neptune

Of course, entering the surreal world of Neptune also exposes us to the less desirable aspects of what is 'not real'. We might encounter deception or manipulation.

The minute we open up, we are vulnerable to all that is out there. When our physical defence barrier and emotional guard are down, we can feel drained by psychic viruses or energy vampires, or be defrauded by fake presentation. We are vulnerable to being let down and disappointed. Our emotional insurance policy must be to sharpen our powers of discrimination so that we don't make ourselves available to these kinds of situations or people. To be trusting is a wonderful thing. To trust with discernment is even better! Otherwise, we can be fooled, taken for a ride.

 A life without suffering in any way, shape or form isn't possible – it's written into our soul contract. Yet we have choices and we need to exercise them.

Creative Magic

Neptune is the special effects department. This is where glamour is created, where fairy dust is sprinkled over people and places, transforming the ordinary into the magical, just like Hollywood. Neptune is the muse for any kind of creativity, but has a true affinity with music, photography and film.

 The language of Neptune is spoken in images.

This is the world of imagination, where a little bit of sparkle lifts the banal into the beautiful. This isn't Venus's type of beauty – the attractive appearance. It is beauty that speaks to the heart. That touches us, melts us. We can be swept up into the atmosphere and aura of it. Neptune can even provide escapism from the everyday realm, transporting us to the astral plane, to the spiritual realm. We get there through the dream-state, meditation, music and beautiful images. It is an elevation for our spirit and feels so pure and transcendent it renders the earthly plane just plain!

Romancing the Soul

With Neptune in the picture, we are filled with longing, yearning. We idealize and fantasize. What we glimpse may have nothing to do with the real world, or the real person, as opposed to our perception and projection of them.

Neptune's essence is the opposite of the ego, as its frequency is encoded with giving rather than taking. So we may believe it's noble to suffer in the name of love, or to rescue someone. We may long for a person who is essentially unavailable and be in love with our idea of them rather than seeing the reality of the relationship.

Things can get messy, confused or even addictive – all portals of escape from the stark reality of what actually is, rather than what we wish it to be. If we delude ourselves or become addicted to external promises of ecstasy, in search of the elusive high, then we are setting ourselves up for a crash. The fantasy of false perfection always leads to dissatisfaction and disappointment.

> *Idealization is a sure sign that we're not engaging with the real person.*

We have to be responsible for choosing carefully and bringing our conscious selves to a relationship! Tuning into Neptune's insight, emotional intelligence and inner knowing will steer us in the right direction.

Neptune as Grace

As we have seen, we can experience loss through Neptune's illusions and delusions. The edges of reality are blurred and we enter misty and mystical territory where we can't 'see' with 20/20 vision. In this place, we are easily manipulated if we don't retain our conscious awareness. Yet these scenarios can teach us powerful lessons about how important it is to hope for the best yet guard against the worst in human nature. What Neptune offers us when we are able to surrender to what we experience, instead of struggling against it, is a state of grace.

This is a rare gift – an awareness that is completely different from anything the machinations of the ego can give us.

> *No matter what has happened, we can decide to take the view that 'everything is perfect' in terms of our soul's journey.*

Neptune Waves of Consciousness

The Generational Wave

Neptune moves very slowly, taking approximately 165 years to circle the zodiac. It spends around 14 years in each sign. This is how it is expressed:

Neptune in Virgo ♍
Personal sacrifice whilst holding hope and vision.

Neptune in Libra ♎
Longing for love.

Neptune in Scorpio ♏
Creative vision for transforming the world.

Neptune in Sagittarius ♐
International and space travel open up new possibilities.

Neptune in Capricorn ♑
Millennials question the establishment.

Neptune in Aquarius ♒
New technology manifests the millennial and Gen-Z mindset.

Neptune in Pisces ♓
The star-seed generation is embedded with fifth-dimensional awareness.

Aspects to the Personal Planets

Neptune–Sun

You are a true Neptunian if you have a major aspect between the Sun and Neptune in your natal chart. You have come into this life with extra sensitivity and empathic awareness, an intuitive sense of who people are. Gentle and unassuming, you'll flow along the path of creativity, healing, spirituality and giving, rather than the ego feed you see around you. You know you're on a different frequency from the taker mentality and need to protect yourself from psychic predators and losses by establishing healthy boundaries. It's important to try to strengthen your ego, as you need to guard against losing yourself in other people. Some aspect of Neptune needs to be incorporated into your identity in order for you to feel whole. But beauty, music, love and spirituality touch your soul.

Neptune–Moon

When the Moon and Neptune are linked in your birth chart, your strongly intuitive nature acts like a psychic radar. Your acute sensitivity opens you up, so you literally feel everything. You soak up other people's feelings and have an in-built desire to heal pain. You're an emotional 'first responder', a person who puts the needs of others before your own, yet possesses a close connection to Source and the realm of creative inspiration. You long for union and fusion and are naturally attuned to how images, atmosphere and the quantum field create space for greater connection.

Neptune–Mercury

You're likely to process information in a highly intuitive way, rather than through logic and reason. This can make some educational subjects more challenging, as logic doesn't make sense to you!

Yet you have stellar powers of perception and imagination. Your mind is attuned to images and creativity. You can lose yourself in a dream world and access incredible inspiration. Not to mention your psychic powers... You can literally read people and/or know what's going to happen. Multidimensional reality is your constant source of guidance.

Neptune–Venus
Venus and Neptune aspects are the rose-coloured spectacles of romance. Not for you the transactional relationship mode. It's all about soul-mates, and you're not averse to a bit of suffering in the name of love. Flowing with sensitivity and wearing your heart on your sleeve, you have so much to give. Ultimately, the higher qualities of love, such as grace and acceptance, are your soul work. Your love pathway may teach you about the necessity of discernment, yet also offer up the possibility of refining what love means. You can grasp the nature of unconditional love, yet need to strengthen your own self in order to hold the potential transcendence of this aspect. A great sensitivity to the arts and beauty can help you appreciate and create.

Neptune–Mars
Your soul code is imprinted with a desire to reach out to other people and engage with higher energies such as compassion, service and creativity. Certainly you'll need to find some uplift beyond the mundane ordinariness of life on the material level. Satisfying the personal ego isn't enough. You have a vision that lies beyond the personal self. You can channel creative inspiration, make a difference to the world, pick up on and respond to trends and longings in the *zeitgeist*. Maintaining a strong sense of your

own desires is important, or you may find yourself giving too much of your vital life energy to others.

CHAPTER 13

Pluto

Power, resourcefulness, transforming the shadow

How do I transform?
How do I access my real power?

Pluto's (♇ in your chart) aura is extreme. Its purpose is to initiate us and wake us up to our true power, a sure-fire way of unlocking our cosmic potential.

What is Power?

The ego and the soul have very different ideas about the true nature of power. Whilst the small ego might want to accumulate material objects that are invested with power, or hold positions of influence over others, the soul is more interested in developing resilience, finding truth and achieving transformation. Since all earthly power is only temporary and we repeatedly see 'how the mighty have fallen', it seems unwise to focus our desires for power on the material plane. Yet the ego is convinced that if we get the right job, house, status, and so on, then somehow we will be immune from the slings and arrows of outrageous fortune!

Attuning ourselves to the nature of real inner power is crucial for living a high-vibration life.

Giving Our Power Away

We may feel we don't possess real power because we habitually give it away at every opportunity. There might be a pay-off for us in doing so, because we don't have to accept the responsibility of becoming empowered. We allow others to make our choices for us and therefore we can blame them for everything and stay in the loop of low self-esteem. This can happen unconsciously. Yet remaining unconscious is one of the biggest power giveaways of all time! If we feel we don't have a choice, then alarm bells should start ringing. *Because we always have a choice.*

How do we get into the position of believing we don't have a choice? More importantly, what keeps us there? Reclaiming our power means we need to get clear about what's happening.

We need to ask ourselves some questions:

- How do I get triggered into giving my power away?
- What kinds of people trip me into doing this?
- What pay-off do I get from conceding my power?
- Is this a pattern from childhood?
- Do I, for instance, have Pluto aspects to personal planets, but attract powerful partners who steal my power?

Once we've seen the ~~pattern~~ the next steps are about releasing, clearing and healing ourselves. How can we do that?

Getting the Wake-Up Call

Pluto's realm is the underworld, and of course few people want to go there voluntarily! In the Hades myth, Persephone is an innocent maiden who walks through the meadows when she is abducted and taken to an underground land. In keeping with his mythological counterpart, Pluto scoops us up and takes us (usually unwillingly) into an encounter with a situation or a relationship where we face things that are far darker than we would have chosen.

 This 'initiation' can feel like an act of fate, a terrible mistake, an unfair encounter or outcome.

But what better way to wake us up to our true power than to place us in the gladiator's ring? Persephone is stripped of her old life. Yet she is destined to become Queen of the Underworld, to discover her own power and to return transformed, with the wisdom to view life on a deeper level. The myth has her then moving regularly between 'normal' life and her deeper terrain, symbolizing the integration of the 'ordinary' with superpower awareness.

 Accepting our initiation is key to our empowerment.

Seeing in the Dark of a Crisis

If we expect life to be inherently fair, then we have more trouble getting in touch with the riches and opportunities inherent in the challenges we are thrown. In the hands of the psychological predator, energy vampire or perpetrator of betrayal, we need to accustom our eyes to the dark. We're in a crisis and bereft of our bearings. The usual ways out won't work, so we have to call up something from deep within.

Pluto's intensity can activate powerful emotions in us. We pass through the natural stages of crisis – denial, bargaining, rage, grief and acceptance – and only in the acceptance phase do we get to see the treasure in this situation. It's only when we stop railing against what's happening that we are able to see that the crisis is actually a gateway to higher consciousness. This won't work if all we want is our old life back. There is no going back from these kinds of experiences. They are designed to transform us and ultimately empower us.

Pluto takes us to a place where we need to do some shadow-dancing, to look at our own or someone else's dark side and our own part in the dynamic. With Pluto, we're exposed to stark black and white, good and bad, dark and light – it's a strong duality. But being able to look at the contrasts without giving in to fear is a massive step forward.

What looks on the outside to be devastation can actually contain a gift for us.

 The capacity to see things differently is a vital step towards transformation.

Accessing Our Soul-Power

Willingness to destroy our own obsolete behaviour patterns is paramount. Clearing those old patterns means we develop a new respect for our personal power. We press the 'refresh' button and drop our attachment to the past. This in itself allows for the possibility of a miracle change. When we are kicking and screaming against what's happening, we create greater tension, resistance and agony. All our attachments and resentments prevent us from moving on. And the crazy thing is that holding on takes up so much more psychic energy than letting go!

But once we release the past, we enter the present, where all the power lies.

 It's a turning point when we are able to receive Pluto's healing inner code as a transmission of our own power.

From here, we can get rid of all the disempowering messages we have built into our psyche. We're capable of changing our own behaviour patterns and realizing that wanting someone else to take care of us only lessens our direct line to our own power.

When we give power to others, we're not in charge of our own domain. When we repeat the stories of what we've been through or stay stuck in what happened, we're losing power all the time. When we take our power back, we activate the light within us. This can mean cutting cords with certain people, but importantly it means cutting cords with the old story, so it simply runs out of juice. We believe other people have betrayed us, and on one level perhaps they have, but if we stay in that story we betray ourselves. Don't contradict the power of your own soul!

Stay in your power and be aware of your choices at every step.

The most important aspect of Pluto is that we are able to heal from whatever is served up to us in our soul contract. Staying stuck in the pain and suffering is actually a device of the ego, because really we can't be destroyed by anything outside us.

It's all an inside job – the soul contract, the power of choice and the healing! When we really take this in, we'll be free to be who we are really here to become.

Waking up, becoming conscious and not pressing the snooze button is our portal to awakening and personal regeneration. What really matters is how well we live our life in the now. The choices we make based on the lesson we've learned and our gift of awareness steer us onto an eternal and internally powerful pathway.

Transformation and Alchemy

Although Pluto's aspects and transits frequently bring us face to face with the lower self, the survival instincts of the lower-frequency ego, the fifth-dimensional energies of grace and surrender can only be accessed by the soul and Higher Self. So, though it feels counter-intuitive, the most empowering thing we can do in a crisis is let go. Let go of the way we think things should be, the person we thought we were and the fear of the unknown (a form of death anxiety). Our ego won't like it, of course, but our soul is arranging for us to receive a huge gift hidden in this crisis. Sometimes we have to make a descent (remember Persephone's time in the underworld) where all feels dark, yet on a soul level, holding the thought that there is nothing wrong keeps that spark of light alive. A psychological death is part of Pluto's pathway to rebirth. Instead of dwelling on what's happening, during the crisis point, we can focus on the *meaning* of it.

When we realize it's a rebirth, the alchemy of the healing begins to work. We can choose to stay aligned with everything that is life-affirming. Our internal resourcefulness and resilience, the hallmarks of our power, will help us stream through the higher-frequency qualities such as love, presence, acceptance, compassion and gratitude. Once we surface from a black hole or a void space, we move into a personal renaissance and our trust and faith in life come back stronger. We don't get caught up in fear. We feel purged and purified, as the universe has gifted us a huge emotional and psychic detox.

 The phoenix rises to a higher frequency.

Pluto's Generational Destiny

The Sign of Our Times

Pluto spends between 12 and 21 years in each sign and takes approximately 248 years to make a complete circuit of the zodiac. These are its areas of focus in each sign:

Pluto in Cancer ♋

Female power and transformation in family life.

Pluto in Leo ♌

The power of the individual spirit.

Pluto in Virgo ♍

Transformation in healthcare and the environment.

Pluto in Libra ♎

Powerful developments in sexual equality, relationships.

Pluto in Scorpio ♏

The AIDS virus, end of apartheid, personal empowerment.

Pluto in Sagittarius ♐

Cultural clashes – the war on terror.

Pluto in Capricorn ♑

Challenges to social, political and economic structures.

Pluto in Aquarius ♒

Freedom of the individual, human rights.

Aspects to the Personal Planets

Pluto–Sun

With this aspect, you're being asked to plug into powerful Pluto in the very essence of your being. You need to believe in your own power. Sun–Pluto people often hide their power, yet radiate it out at an unconscious level. Other people sense your strength, which is contained until it's activated by a power surge to regain personal control. Some aspects between Pluto and the Sun operate as projection: you attract powerful others to catalyze you to find the power in yourself. Your life path demands you personally transform and find your power place.

Pluto–Moon

Aspects between Moon and Pluto point to deeply hidden and unconscious feelings. When the god of the underworld connects with your tender Moon, your emotional security may have been challenged in your early years. Learning to open up and trust others is a major part of your healing journey, as you're naturally self-protective. Your emotional nature is deep, intense and complex, yet offers scope for powerful emotional intelligence and regeneration.

Pluto–Mercury

These aspects offer deep perception. You're a natural investigator and possess powerful instincts and thought processes that yield tremendous insight into what lies beneath the surface. You're a truth seeker. You pick up on the invisible signals that others cannot see and your powers of analysis and desire to know make you psychologically adept at reading people and situations.

Pluto–Venus

With these aspects, your relationships are soul-stamped with a need to discover the true power of love. Nothing superficial will do. You might be drawn to a complex person, or the relationship itself may deliver eye-opening lessons. You seek passion and intensity, ranging from the deeply physical to the deepest love. Along the way, it's possible that you're going to get the true Persephone experience of being initiated into reclaiming your power through the catalyst of relationship. It's also possible that other Venusian areas, such as your values, creativity or relationship to the feminine, are going to bring up depth-charged experiences and require resourcefulness and deep awareness.

Pluto–Mars

Still waters run deep with you. To the outside world, your power, endurance, drive and resilience might not be obvious. But scratch the surface, or cross you, and your strength emerges. You may find your personal will is controlled or subdued in earlier years, leading to paralysis rather than self-assertion. There can be a fear of the shadow, a desire to placate and please others. Yet at some point you're going to be challenged to use your willpower to overcome resistance or difficulty. Your soul wants you to raise the frequency of the yang, masculine force.

Flowing with the Cosmos

Now you have a map showing your soul design, your life path, what's going on for you and how you can be in a state of exquisite flow with the cosmos. My wish is that you have some incredible insights into who you really are and who you can be.

The cosmos guides and supports us in our growth – the universe and the soul wish to collaborate. But sometimes we don't know how to listen. Or we want everything on our terms – the terms of the small ego. If we can wake up and realize we have the power to transform, we are taken to the next level in our evolution.

When we know our astrological blueprint, we get a super-charged connection with the cosmos. We start collaborating. We start inhabiting a metaphysical world that bridges the human and the divine. We can dialogue with the cosmos and have a conscious conversation. We can manifest this new awareness from our soul in the material world.

The wisdom of our celestial signature gives us the power of our spiritual self. It helps write our graceful and meaningful future. Flow with the cosmos into that high frequency future now.

Glossary of Astrological Terms

Air Sign
Gemini, Libra, Aquarius

Angle
Ascendant (AC), Imum Coeli (I/C), Descendant (DC), Midheaven (MC)

Ascendant (AC)
Also known as the Rising Sign, is the sign that is on the horizon point at your time, date and place of birth.

Aspect
The angles the planets make to each other which define their relationship to each other.

Birth Chart
A chart or circular map which shows the positions of the planets and angles created by the time, date and place of your birth.

Conjunction
Planets that are close together in your birth chart, usually within 10 degrees, which blends their themes together.

Descendant (DC)
The sign that is setting at the time, date and place of your birth and marks the 7th house (relationship).

Earth Sign
Taurus, Virgo, Capricorn

Fire Sign
Aries, Leo, Sagittarius

House
A segment within your birth chart wheel that denotes a specific area of life.

Imum Coeli (I/C)
The point at the bottom of your astrological chart which marks the 4th house.

Law of Attraction
The idea that you attract what you think, either consciously or unconsciously.

Midheaven (M/C)
The point at the top of your birth chart that marks the 10th House.

Node
A point on the chart calculated by the Moon's interception of the ecliptic. Both the North and South Node are associated with our destiny and soul journey.

Outer Planets
Uranus, Neptune, Pluto

Personal Planets
Sun, Moon (celestial bodies or luminaries), Mercury, Venus, Mars

Planetary Sign
The astrological sign in which a planet is placed at the time, date and place of your birth.

Retrograde
When a planet appears to reverse in the heavens for a period of time during its orbit of the Sun.

Saturn Return
When Saturn returns to the place in your birth chart where it was when you were born (every 29 years).

Social Planets
Jupiter and Saturn

Transit
The cycles and movements of the planets in their orbits interpreted in relation to your birth chart.

Water Signs
Cancer, Scorpio, Pisces

Further Reading

Stephen Arroyo, *Astrology, Psychology and the Four Elements: An Energy Approach to Astrology and Its Use in the Counselling Arts*, CRCS Publications, 1984

Debbie Frank, *Written in the Stars: Discover the Language of the Stars and Help Your Life Shine*, Headline, 2018

Liz Greene and Howard Sasportas, *The Luminaries: The Psychology of the Sun and Moon in the Horoscope*, Red Wheel/Weiser, 1992

Liz Greene and Howard Sasportas, *The Inner Planets: Building Blocks of Personal Reality*, Red Wheel/Weiser, 1993

Babs Kirby and Janey Stubbs, *Love and Sexuality: An Exploration of Venus and Mars*, Element Books, 1992

Tracy Marks, *The Astrology of Self-Discovery: An In-depth Exploration of the Potentials Revealed in Your Birth Chart*, CRCS Publications, 1986

Howard Sasportas, *The Twelve Houses: Exploring the Houses of the Horoscope*, Flare Publications, 1985

Sue Tompkins, *Aspects in Astrology: A Comprehensive Guide to Interpretation*, Element Books, 1989; Rider Books, 2001

Acknowledgements

Heartfelt thanks to Ileen Maisel, Michelle Pilley and Kezia Bayard-White, who were instrumental in bringing this book about.

Also, many thanks to the entire talented team at Hay House and very personally to my mentor and teacher, Dr Yubraj Sharma.

About the Author

Debbie Frank is a world-renowned Master Astrologer with decades of experience in sharing, teaching and providing life healing to her personal clients, celebrities, CEOs and royalty (she was Princess Diana's personal astrologer from 1989 onwards).

Debbie's training in psychological and spiritual astrology provides her clients with mentoring, meaning and life direction via a combination of her astrological insights, bespoke meditations and healing modalities.

Debbie is the author of *Birth Signs, Baby Signs, Cosmic Ordering Guide to Life, Love and Happiness, Written in the Stars* and *Soul Signs*. She is a much-loved media astrologer around the globe and has written for publications including *Instyle*, the *Mail Online*, *People* magazine's *Royals* edition, the *Daily Mirror, Sunday Mirror* and *The Sun*. She is currently the astrological features writer for *Hello! Magazine* online and the *Sun on Sunday* and her insights are much sought after as a contributor to TV documentaries on the royals.

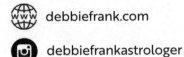

debbiefrank.com

debbiefrankastrologer

We hope you enjoyed this Hay House book. If you'd like to receive our online catalog featuring additional information on Hay House books and products, or if you'd like to find out more about the Hay Foundation, please contact:

Hay House LLC, P.O. Box 5100, Carlsbad, CA 92018-5100
(760) 431-7695 or (800) 654-5126
www.hayhouse.com® • www.hayfoundation.org

———

Published in Australia by:
Hay House Australia Publishing Pty Ltd
18/36 Ralph St., Alexandria NSW 2015
Phone: +61 (02) 9669 4299
www.hayhouse.com.au

Published in the United Kingdom by:
Hay House UK Ltd
The Sixth Floor, Watson House,
54 Baker Street, London W1U 7BU
Phone: +44 (0) 203 927 7290
www.hayhouse.co.uk

Published in India by:
Hay House Publishers (India) Pvt Ltd
Muskaan Complex, Plot No. 3,
B-2, Vasant Kunj, New Delhi 110 070
Phone: +91 11 41761620
www.hayhouse.co.in

———

Access New Knowledge.
Anytime. Anywhere.

Learn and evolve at your own pace
with the world's leading experts.

www.hayhouseU.com